BEST PRACTICES

OF GROWING CHURCHES

PROFILES AND CONVERSATIONS WITH MINISTRY LEADERS

voices

BEST PRACTICES

OF GROWING CHURCHES

PROFILES AND CONVERSATIONS
WITH MINISTRY LEADERS

Tom Nees

BEACON HILL PRESS
OF KANSAS CITY

Copyright 2007

by Tom Nees and Beacon Hill Press of Kansas City

ISBN 978-0-8341-2304-5

Printed in the
United States of America

Cover Design: Chad A. Cherry

Cover Photo: Don Pluff

Interior Design: Sharon Page

Library of Congress Cataloging-in-Publication Data

Nees, Thomas G., 1937-
    Best practices of growing churches : profiles and conversations with ministry leaders / Tom
Nees.
        p. cm.
    Includes bibliographical references.
    ISBN 978-0-8341-2304-5 (pbk.)
    1. Church growth. 2. Big churches. 3. Church work. 4. Christian leadership. I. Title.

    BV652.25.N44 2007
    254'.50973—dc22

                                                                                2007041389

10 9 8 7 6 5 4 3 2 1

CONTENTS

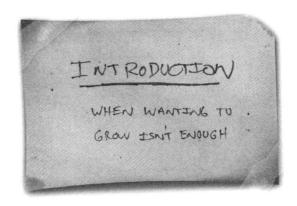

INTRODUCTION

WHEN WANTING TO GROW ISN'T ENOUGH

It's not an easy time to grow a church. Addressing Nazarene clergy in a series of conferences in 2004, George G. Hunter, professor of evangelism and church growth at Asbury Theological Seminary, claimed that when compared with population growth, 80 percent of churches have plateaued or are declining.[1] That is true for Evangelical denominations as well as for mainline churches.

Church culture is extremely competitive. Most people drive by several churches to reach their home church. Add church television and radio, the constant stream of religious books, and now the Internet, and it's clear that people have many options to meet their spiritual needs. No one has to go to church or put money in the offering. It's all voluntary, and alternatives are endless.

Churches compete with each other for the attention and time of increasingly busy people who are often reluctant to commit themselves to membership as they shop for a place that meets their needs. For some people, going to just one church is not enough. Pastors tell of those who attend, or even join, more than one church, picking and choosing among several churches depending upon the program that most suits their needs at the moment.

Several denominational studies confirm the view of church consultants—such as George Barna, leader of the Barna Group <www.barna.org>, and John Vaughan, director of Church Growth Today <www.churchgrowthtoday.org>—that church attendance in the United States and Canada is on the decline, with fewer than 20 percent of the general population in church on a given Sunday.

Pastors know that active members seldom attend or even intend to attend church every Sunday. Thus it takes more members to maintain the same average attendance as in the past. The growing churches I've visited would suggest that a lot of people still want to go to church but not church as it has been done in the past.

Even though not all large churches are growing, the trend is toward the concentration of more people, and thus money, in fewer larger churches. While some medium and small churches are doing quite well, the offerings are not enough in many of them to support a wide range of programs for children and youth along with worship experiences led by professional-sounding musicians.

Churched as well as unchurched people view churches and denominations different from the past. Denominational identity and loyalty is eroding. In his book *The Present Future: Six Tough Questions for the Church*,[2] Reggie McNeal claims that the traditional church with its emphasis on numbers and dollars is a spent force, not worth propping up. He suggests that churches should be evaluated by the redemptive effect they have on their neighborhoods rather than their size and wealth.

Barna's book *Revolution*[3] documents a mass exodus of true believers from local churches. He claims that these church dropouts are highly committed to the Christian faith, stewardship, and missions. They are choosing to live out their faith in a variety of alternative gatherings without the infrastructure and expectations placed on church members by denominations and local congregations.

There was a time when church growth was more or less spontaneous. It's different now. Sustainable growth requires strategic planning and the implementation of programs that meet the unique needs of individuals, families in various subcultures, and people groups. The Church Growth Movement began in the mid-20th century with a desire to apply successful missionary strategies from other continents and countries to the United States as presented in Donald McGavran's book *Bridges of God*. Since then shelves of books, hundreds of conferences, and publications such as the *Journal of the American Society for Church Growth* have tried to inform church leaders about how to start and grow churches.

And yet, with all these resources, books, conferences, and strategic plans, the decline in the rate of growth, if not an absolute decline in church membership and attendance, continues in the United States and Canada.

It's not that all churches have plateaued or are declining. It's just that the losses from declining churches are more than the gains of growing churches. Paul Borden, executive minister of the American Baptist Churches of the West, in *Hit the Bullseye*[4] describes how his jurisdiction of 200 congregations in Northern California and Northern Nevada was transformed from a network of small, mostly declining congregations to a majority of churches with an annual growth rate of 5 percent <www.growinghealthychurches.org>. That's fairly remarkable. In 2006 only 240 (4.7 percent) of the 5,121 Nazarene congregations in the United States and Canada reported 5 percent or more growth for the past three consecutive years. However, 1,213 (23.7 percent) congregations from all size groups reported an average of 5 percent increase or 15 percent for three years.

Even with the many churches that are declining—and likely to close unless they reinvent themselves—it's a mistake to conclude that the church or a particular denomination, such as the Church of the Nazarene in the United States and Canada, is in decline. Many congregations are growing rapidly. Interestingly enough, growing and declining churches of the same tradition can be found side by side in similar neighborhoods and cities.

In their recent book *Simple Church*,[5] Thom Rainer and Eric Geiger identify what they believe is the key to significant, or what they call "vibrant," growth of 5 percent a year. There are many Nazarene churches that report such vibrant growth. Some are adding 100 or more to their membership and attendance annually. Others have doubled in size in the recent past. Is there then something that the majority of churches that have plateaued or are in a multiyear decline can learn from these growing congregations?

How-to books and conferences alone are not the answer. It takes more than following a list of oughts and shoulds to start and grow a church. Working harder and just wanting to grow is not enough. Since most, if not all pastors and churches want to grow in quality or health as well as quantity or fruitfulness, what does it take besides wanting to grow and working harder to succeed?

This book is about learning from others and innovatively adapting strategies needed to produce sustainable growth in local congregations. Through the years I've listened to many explanations for lack of growth or why churches can't grow. Yet in nearly every setting where churches are declining others in similar settings are thriving.

The chapters in the first part of this book are observations from my on-site visits to some of these growing churches that have prospered under the leadership of long-term pastors. The lessons to be learned are referred to as "best practices," a discipline of observing and learning described in the next chapter. The "best practices" described here are not the only ways to do church. There are many right ways. There are thriving churches that don't fit any of the descriptions offered here. However, with all the variety in the emerging church world, I've observed a few patterns or trends in these growing churches.

The second part of this book, Profiles and Conversations, consists of stories of churches and pastors from which there is much to learn. As I asked the selected pastors, as well as many others, about their churches and their personal journeys, I was impressed with the importance each of their stories held as the narrative of the people of God in a particular place and time.

In 2005, a group of Nazarene pastors in a leadership training program were given a tour and orientation to the 10,000-member First Baptist Church in Orlando—a congregation established over 150 years ago. In the foyer of one of their buildings is a mural 20 feet high and over 100 feet long on which is painted the people and events of their 150-year-old story. Visitors to their services are invited to become part of the ongoing story of Orlando First Baptist.

In their book *The Missional Leader*,[6] Alan J. Roxburgh and Fred Romanuk take this a step further. They are training pastors to be turnaround specialists with the skills needed to help declining churches discover and own their own stories. They are convinced that for churches to experience healthy growth, the members must see themselves as part of a story God is writing through them <www.mliweb.net>.

In this book I've selected a few pastors to tell their stories—stories of their leadership over several years with churches that have grown in significance as well as size. By any evaluation these pastors have been very successful. However, few, if any, would equate success with numbers only. They are not satisfied with programs that attract transient visitors who never learn to love God, one another, or get involved with mission. They are as committed to making disciples as they are to making converts.

I. OBSERVATIONS

LEARNING FROM
BEST PRACTICES

In January 2006, Larry Osborne, pastor of the 5,000-member North Coast Church in Vista, California, spoke to a group of Nazarene pastors attending the Large Church Leadership Conference in San Diego. Following his presentation the pastors spent an afternoon at the church campus to learn firsthand about how North Coast goes about its "multisite" ministry. They returned on Sunday morning to attend worship with 6,500 others in one of their several venues.

It's one thing to read about multisite ministry—quite another to hear about it from Osborne and his staff—even better to attend one of their many worship experiences. Pastor Osborne and his staff never suggested that others could do church exactly as they do it, and I don't think any of the Nazarene pastors who were there have tried to duplicate North Coast. And yet, a few pastors have since implemented multisite ministries of their own design. The North Coast experience sparked creative ideas that have been adapted to other settings.

That's an example of learning from best practices—a highly developed methodology in the corporate world. In *Benchmarking for Best Practices: Winning Through Innovative Adaptation*,[1] Christopher Bogan and Michael English describe this learning process as more than a discipline to gain a competitive advantage—it's a personal as well as corporate way of life. It's about developing the skill to learn from others, even from those in very different enterprises. They describe how Henry Ford got his idea for assembly-line production from observing the processing of livestock in a Chicago meatpacking plant.

Since most of the information about benchmarking is for the corporate world only, a few in the nonprofit world and virtually none in the religious community have adapted this discipline to their activities. (A Google search for the words *benchmarking* or *best practices* leads to extensive resources and practices common to corporations and government agencies.)

Even though pastors learn from one another, they do not necessarily understand or apply benchmarking for best practices as a learning discipline. Most books intended to help pastors and churches do well are organized around lists of oughts and shoulds—lists of suggested steps from proven experience that will lead to success, if only applied. As helpful as such books may be, that's not necessarily the way to learn from best practices.

Learning from best practices is learning by observation and (in the subtitle of the book by Bogan and English) implementing "innovative adaptation." It encourages leaders to find comparables such as a pastor might do in finding and observing a growing church of similar size in a similar setting. It's knowing *how* things are done as well as what needs to be done and how to distinguish between what can and cannot be adapted to another setting.

For example, it's more helpful to observe how Pastor Kerry Willis at Harrisonburg First Nazarene has been able to recruit dozens of men as prayer partners than to simply be told that prayer is important in growing churches. Listening to Pastor Willis describe how he used his interest in fishing to lead mean into a prayer fellowship could help other pastors discover ways that they, too, can use their life experiences to connect men to spiritual development.

Pastors of many growing churches will tell you that worship must have flow. I can describe flow as an experience where several components (music, prayer, preaching, drama, video, etc.) are combined and blended into a seamless experience of worship. But I didn't really understand it until I attended worship at the Valparaiso, Indiana, First Church of the Nazarene, as the next chapter shows.

On his Web site <http://www.bockinfo.com/docs/benchmarking.htm> Wally Bock suggests that learning from best practices "refers to identifying, sharing and implementing practices that result in improvements in either efficiency or effectiveness. Best Practices programs are continuous quests for improvement."

He continues, "To find good practices you need to measure your results and those of others. Then you need to go out and aggressively find out who's doing good things. Your business intelligence efforts should help you find out what's being done by others."

For the last 15 years, through the Church of the Nazarene K-Church training program (churches with average attendance of 250 or more), pastors have learned from the best practices of churches from various traditions and now some of them are teaching others. They've overcome one of the impediments that stand in the way of learning from best practices—that is, being threatened by the success of others. In the church world, competition often results in resentment rather than learning. At their best, pastors and churches are collaborators, not competitors. I've found that pastors of growing churches are more than willing to share their experiences and give their time to teach others.

Ed Stetzer and David Putman in their recent book *Breaking the Missional Code* suggest that pastors and members of churches seeking to revitalize themselves find and visit growing churches. Some growing churches such as the Grove City, Ohio, Church of the

Nazarene—the largest Nazarene church in the United States, with a 3,500-average attendance—sponsors conferences to which pastors and leaders of many denominations are invited <www.grovecity-nazarene.org>. The First Church of the Nazarene in Colorado Springs is a teaching church where Pastor Gene Grate leads growth seminars and provides comprehensive resources through "The Minister's Tool Box" <www.realliferesources.org>.

After many years of training denominational leaders and pastors through the United States/Canada Mission/Evangelism Department <www.usacanadamission.org>, we have found that pastors learn best from peer-to-peer learning linked with coaching and mentoring. Learning how to innovate and adapt from the best practices of growing churches is a proven strategy for starting and revitalizing churches.

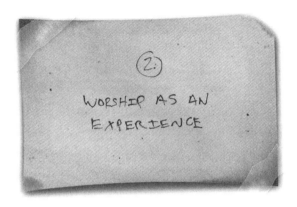

2.

WORSHIP AS AN EXPERIENCE

When we visited the Salem Fields Church of the Nazarene in Fredericksburg, Virginia, my wife and I were first greeted in the parking lot and then again at the entrance to the worship center, where we were introduced to a hostess who escorted us to our seats during a service in progress. We weren't asked if we were visitors or guests. Everyone gets treated this way at Salem Fields <www.salem-fields.com>.

I've found that in larger growing churches with multiple services it's sometimes difficult to identify visitors. Hospitality is extended to everyone. At the Church on the Hill in McMinnville, Oregon <www.hillchurch.com>, I learned from Pastor Jerry Moen that the best question to ask someone who you don't recognize is "How long have you been attending here?" He suggests that you don't want to embarrass yourself and inadvertently offend others—perhaps members—by asking if they're visitors. The question "How long have you been attending here?" is always welcomed and, as I've found, usually begins very interesting conversations.

Growing churches plan worship as a means of evangelism to attract visitors as well as nurture the members. Worship has become a mission-driven experience led by worship leaders who do much more than direct choirs and lead congregational singing. They facilitate an integrated flow of activities, including high-energy music typically with a Christian rock band in addition to, or more often in place of, the typical sound of a church organ and piano. Video projection of words and images have all but replaced hymn books and printed orders of worship.

Growing churches are finding ways of satisfying the varying music and worship preferences of their members as they appeal to visitors. Some churches have developed a blended style that is repeated in multiple services, while others will offer choices, usually referred to as traditional and contemporary. Darrel Wiseman, while pastor of the Marley Park Church of the Nazarene near Baltimore (now at Boise First), said that it's all about the "sound of music." At Marley Park he led three services—each with a different sound. The drum service was Saturday night, the keyboard service was early Sunday, with the traditional organ and piano sound at 11 A.M. He preached the same message in each service. Pastor Ian Robertson at Spokane Valley started a Saturday night "oldies but goodies" service for seniors where it's OK to sing hymns—even sitting rather standing and clapping through unfamiliar choruses. This is more than an accommodation to older members who can't change. It's an intentional strategy to retain and minister to a lot of people who still like traditional worship.

Pine and Gilmore, authors of *The Experience Economy: Work Is Theatre and Every Business a Stage,*[1] have taught pastors and other church leaders to adapt business "experience economy" strategies to the faith community <www.strategichorizons.com>. In their book they explain why, for instance, we're willing to pay so much for a cup of coffee at Starbucks. We're not just buying coffee—we're paying for an experience. Pastors of growing churches know that people want more than a worship service. They want a worship experience.

The Sunday worship experience at Valparaiso First Church of the Nazarene is worship as theater. It has the recognizable components of traditional worship—congregational singing, choirs, prayer at the altar, offerings, preaching with an invitation to come to faith—but it's all choreographed with carefully planned sight and sound. There were more that 20 light changes during the service I attended. I discovered that their lighting control board is as large as the sound board. Their worship planning committee understands the importance of staging with good sound and light systems.

On the Sunday morning I attended, I sat behind a family with children and teens who were as attentive as their parents. They were absorbed in the compelling progression of high energy music from the band and choir, a video clip from Rob Bell's Nooma <www.nooma.org> resources, actors performing onstage, and a dramatic sermon from Pastor Tanner. It was not boring or predictable. The sanctuary was filled with families. People of all ages were caught up in the experience.

Worship experiences like this are the point of entry for most visitors to growing churches. While these churches have multiple programs that attract and involve new people, growing churches know that their members are more likely to invite friends to a vibrant worship service than any other activity. In a conference sponsored by the Leadership Network <www.leadnet.org> I heard Pastor Larry Osborne of the 6,000-member North Coast Church in Vista, California, say that all of their growth is the result of word-of-mouth invitations. A Web site is their only advertising <www.north-coastchurch.com>.

Osborne went on to comment that pastors should know that if their members are not inviting and bringing their friends to worship, it means they're "mildly embarrassed" about what's going on. They may attend regularly out of commitment, but they're not excited enough to tell others about it.

In growing churches, weekend worship is planned as a mission to lead people to faith as well as a time for members to be nurtured through singing, Scripture reading, sacraments, and preaching. Sunday evening evangelism services have been all but abandoned for one primary weekend worship experience, often repeated at different times and places. These vibrant, engaging worship experiences have become the most effective gateway to evangelism and discipleship in growing congregations. According to Rainer and Geiger, it's the time and place most unchurched visitors come to know and love God. At Valparaiso First Nazarene, Pastor Gene Tanner wants each service to create a buzz in the parking lot. On their way out he likes to hear comments such as, "That was really good"—meaning you don't want to miss Sunday because each service is an experience not to be repeated.

With worship arts committees, worship leaders begin planning months in advance. They most often begin with preaching themes and then add ideas from musicians, stage set designers, audio/video and lighting technicians, children's and youth leaders, and dramatists. At Valpo—Valparaiso First Nazarene—after six months or more of planning, the worship participants rehearse for Sunday on Thursday evening and meet on Monday to debrief.

Worship as an experience has dramatically changed the sound, look, and feel of worship. Platforms have become stages for sets designed especially to create ambiance. Pulpits have been replaced with simple podiums or have been removed altogether as pastors have become comfortable speaking without notes, using only a handheld or lapel mike. Worship participants, including pastors and musicians, sit near the front rather than on the platform until their time comes to participate. Everything is carefully designed to eliminate anything that might distract from direct connection to and effective communication with the congregation.

New styles of worship are changing church architecture. At Yuba

City Nazarene—YCN—the original modern church building nearest the main road has been retrofitted for a children's ministry center. A larger worship center was recently constructed behind the former church building. The new worship center building is a large multipurpose rectangle box with 750 padded chairs that can be arranged as needed to face the stage on the long side of the auditorium. The building has no windows, making it possible to enhance the worship experience with multiple lighting changes and dramatic videos on the large screens on either side of the stage <www.ycnaz.org>. Sanctuaries with pews, stained-glass windows, and organs and pianos are giving way to buildings that resemble concert halls or theaters with high-tech sound systems and stages large enough to accommodate bands, choirs, and drama.

Preaching is changing as well. For the most part oratory is gone. I asked Pastor Jerry Moen to describe his preaching style. He replied that he doesn't preach. He has, he said, a conversation with 2,000 people. I've found pastors of growing churches to be very good communicators who generally begin planning their preaching schedules months, if not a year or so, in advance. But they know that people don't like being preached at. The wagging finger is gone. They've learned to communicate for an immediate, natural connection with the audience. Ideally they want an auditorium where they can make eye contact even with people in the back rows. I've seen platforms with built-out extensions to provide close contact with the audience. It's not uncommon for preachers to leave the platform altogether and speak from the same level as the congregation.

The preaching style in a worship experience is sometimes like a standup comedian or perhaps like Wayne Dwyer, the self-help, positive-thinking guru seen on public television. Like Dwyer, they are well prepared and skilled at improvisation. They can spontaneously pick up on something unexpected or move with the response of the audience. Pastor Dan Huckins at the Lima Community Church in

Lima, Ohio, walks around the platform as he preaches, occasionally returning to a small waist-high round table where he places his Bible and notes. It has the look and feel of a conversation one might have in the comfort and intimacy of home.

Most growing churches make extensive use of video projection on one or more screens, with PowerPoint slides for scripture and teaching notes and video clips during the message as well as at other times in the service.

In most of the growing English-speaking white churches I've visited, the dress code is casual. Very few people, including the pastors, wear suits and ties anymore. This, too, is a part of communication. Casual dress sends an intentional message to the target audience that people are welcome to come to church as they are. It's a nonverbal way of connecting with people who might feel uncomfortable if they're not dressed up. Jerry Moen jokes that his attendance increased by 100 when he quit tucking in his shirt. At the Pismo Beach, California, Community Church of the Nazarene, Ron Salsbury dresses and communicates to connect with his California beach town. He admits that his style would not work in other places. Whatever the setting, the message of casual dress is part of an attempt to achieve transparency, to demonstrate that the preacher and church members are approachable to one another as well their target audience.

It's quite different, however, among some people groups where even the poor will wear their best to church. It's expected that the preacher dress up out of respect, not only for the Lord but to honor the people.

Worship experiences are now being informed as much by the media as by traditions handed down through generations of religious practice. The Sunday School teacher in an adult class I attended while visiting a growing church mentioned something he'd heard on Andy Stanley's TV church. I wondered what he thought about his own church service after watching Andy Stanley. Pastors of growing churches know that while they can't and shouldn't try to compete with megachurch television preachers, they must plan, prepare, and evaluate to create quality worship experiences of their own.

People will drive across town for a good meal or a good worship experience. In our experience-driven culture it takes more than just a good sermon to attract and retain people. There are many other components to a quality worship experience if it is to be an effective mission, helping people come to know and love God.

3.

ORGANIZING FOR
GROWTH

A few years ago I attended a K-Church conference for pastors of churches averaging over 250 who wanted to reach 1,000 in attendance. One of the most popular seminars was conducted by Rev. Bobby Huffaker, then pastor of the Grove City Church of the Nazarene. As mentioned earlier, with a worship attendance of 3,000 plus it was, and still is, the largest Nazarene congregation in the United States.

The presentation and discussion was on the topic Board-Driven vs. Staff-Driven Churches. Since the number of Nazarene churches with attendance of 250 or more is increasing, there has been a significant increase in staff positions. Pastor Huffaker described how the significant growth at Grove City required reorganizing the church, particularly the church board, as paid staff members were added.

He was one of the first to move from a board-driven to a staff-driven structure. The board was reduced to nine members and elected as a group rather than as trustees and stewards. Each board member was assigned to a standing committee (children, youth, building development, personnel, finance, etc.) chaired by a staff member. These committees, including other appointed members, were given responsibility for managing a budget appropriated for their particular ministry. The committees met monthly, while the full board met quarterly, primarily to review committee reports and to encourage the entire congregation to healthy growth.

Large growing churches such as Grove City are employing executive pastors to oversee day-by-day activities, convene staff meetings, and manage finances. Executive pastors are expected to help release the senior pastor from operational details to give more time to top level leadership and preaching responsibilities.

Pastors of growing churches know they must organize or reorganize their churches for growth. While traditional church boards may do a good job of managing small churches, unless they are willing to change they may become an impediment to growth in a larger, growing church. Some pastors now advocate starting new churches with this structure given the difficulty of reorganizing after significant growth begins.

In growing churches, boards are becoming more like the boards of nonprofit organizations where a distinction is made between governance and management. As described in books such as *Boards That Make a Difference*,[1] by John Carver, boards govern; the executive director and staff manage. The primary governance responsibility of a church board is to work with the judicatory leader/district superintendent and the congregation to select and evaluate the senior pastor, who as an executive director or CEO is responsible for managing the church—including hiring (and firing, if need be) staff, and with staff (paid and volunteer) guiding all the programs and ministries, including worship, education, outreach, missions, and building development. The trend is toward smaller, decentralized boards that understand and respect the difference between governance and management.

In his March 2007 presentation to ANSR (Association of Nazarene Sociologists of Religion) Gary McIntosh, president of the American Society for Church Growth, presented a paper, "One Size Doesn't Fit All, or Understanding Size as a Factor in Church Growth," in which he reviewed a wide range of studies on how churches change as they grow. He suggested that small, board-run churches don't need a pastor to manage the church. The programs, ministries, building maintenance, and financial responsibilities of small churches are divided up among the elected board members. All this changes as churches begin to grow. In larger growing churches pastors become highly visible leaders, managing and or-ganizing paid staff and members for congregational care and out-reach. "As a church grows," McIntosh explained, "it cannot simply employ business as usual practices. Larger churches are not simply bigger versions of smaller churches, but in reality an entirely differ-ent structure that requires different operational procedures" <http://media.premierstudios.com/nazarene/docs/OneSize McIntosh2007.pdf>.

Pastors know that in changing the role of the board from man-agement to governance, some board members may sense a loss of importance and control. However, they usually find that the work of governance is as rewarding as it is important and does not pre-clude their involvement in the ministries and activities of the church. Through the committee structures all the board members as well as other willing church members are provided opportunities to serve in areas of their calling and expertise.

Pastors also talk about how they must change their personal leadership style as growth occurs. It's impossible for a senior pastor of a large church to make house calls on everyone, to officiate at all the marriages and funerals, to visit every hospitalized member and friend, or even to baptize all the converts. Increasingly, the members and staff of growing congregations must participate in congregational care rather than depend entirely on the attention of the senior pastor.

While visiting a larger growing church recently, I met my college roommate who was an active member of the Sunday School class I attended. After so many years we didn't recognize one another until I was introduced as a guest. When I told the pastor about my friend, he admitted that he didn't know him. That's not necessarily unusual in a large church. Large churches grow because they are able to create smaller communities through Sunday School classes, cell groups, or any number of other affinity or mission groups within the congregation. In a large church few if any members, including the pastor, know everyone, but everyone can be known by someone or several people in a small group of some sort—that is, if they want to be. One pastor told me that by the time he makes a hospital visit, he's usually been preceded by other members and friends from the church.

On the other hand, some people attend large churches because they want to remain anonymous. When I've asked pastors about the number of visitors who may attend on a given Sunday, they'll usually estimate. All they know is about the ones who identify themselves. They are aware that some visitors avoid providing personal information. They may attend periodically for extended periods of time without wanting to be contacted. They don't want to wear a visitor's ribbon or receive mail, and they certainly don't want an unannounced knock on their door. For these people part of the appeal of a larger church is being able to attend without having to commit.

Pastors know that visitors are understandably tentative about their future participation. When announcing the offering they will sometimes tell visitors that as guests of the congregation they are welcome to attend without financial or any other kind of obligation. The challenge for growing churches is to encourage visitors to become converts and disciples. Even though many do, some do not. Even so, these transient visitors are important since they are likely to tell others who may be more interested in a particular church than they are. You'll never hear Christmas and Easter visitors criticized in a growing church. Every visitor is a potential gateway into the unchurched population outside the church.

In the past it was relatively easy for people to predict what they would encounter upon visiting a church for the first time. The primary activities of most congregations were predictable—Sunday School at 9:45 A.M., morning worship at 11 A.M., Sunday evening worship, Wednesday prayer meeting with youth groups, and other special-interest activities announced during the Sunday services. There was an unstated shared understanding of how churches functioned. Denominational resources—including Sunday School lessons, hymn books, missionary studies, and youth programs—were provided with the assumption that most churches do the same things in the same way.

All this has changed. There is no longer a typical Nazarene, Baptist, or any other kind of church—particularly with growing churches. With multiple service times on Sunday as well as weekday services, congregations now assume the freedom to tailor-make their worship experiences and congregational activities to suit their own unique situations and needs. In addition to what might be considered the essential components of congregational life—worship, religious education, and outreach—growing churches are importing many other programs.

Celebrate Recovery <www.celebraterecovery.com>, Upward Sports <www.upward.org>, MOPS—Mothers of Preschoolers <www.mops.org>, and Alpha <www.alpha.org> are just a few of the parachurch programs I've seen growing churches use to attract and retain visitors. Pastor Jerry Moen at the Church on the Hill has more than 500 people involved in various Celebrate Recovery groups. The leader of this ministry is also the director of the program for the state of Oregon. Pastor Ian Robertson at the Spokane

Valley Church reported more than 200 women attending their weekday MOPS program. Free child care is provided by church members for these mothers for whom this is their only contact with the church. Spokane Valley is the organizing hub for Upward Sports, which now attracts hundreds of youth and parents in several nearby congregations. Pastor Dan Huckins at the Lima, Ohio, Community Church of the Nazarene says that the Alpha program has become his primary means of evangelism and discipleship.

The typical list of activities provided by growing churches includes an extensive menu of programs for all age and interest groups. While the worship experience remains the primary entry point for visitors, the wide selection of programmed activities become magnets for people new to the congregation.

Organizing for growth requires new methods to involve as many people as possible in congregational care and missions. Growth seldom occurs by simply adding more people to existing programs or activities. Someone has said that change is inevitable, improvement is optional. All churches are experiencing change both from within and from without. Growing churches have figured out how to change for the better.

4
REACHING A TARGET AUDIENCE

Growing congregations are alike in at least two ways. First, they are good at congregational care, and second, they have given up what Stetzer and Putman in their book *Breaking the Missional Code* describe as the "sin of preferences." Both are essential. Growing churches need to retain their members and friends even as they implement strategies to attract unchurched people as visitors and potential members.

The challenge for most churches is to make the changes needed for growth without losing the core congregational constituency with its financial support. While pastors of growing churches lament the loss of members, they know that losses are sometimes inevitable and perhaps necessary. How to add more new members than they lose is a very real challenge in our mobile society as some churches need to add 10 to 20 percent a year just to stay even.

Pastor Dwight Gunter has led the Trevecca Community Church of the Nazarene through a significant time of transition and growth without losing the core constituency of his church. His study of transitions without losing people is documented in his doctor of ministry project/thesis at Nazarene Theological Seminary. He has effectively implemented a grow-without-losing strategy at Trevecca

Community. In recent years the church has included a subculture of the Nashville population that would have otherwise been a threat to the congregation.

The members of growing churches I've visited are convinced that they are not the target audience. This may be the most significant distinction between growing and no-growth churches. Growing churches are willing to give up their preferences, or the way they like things done, to remove the barriers—often unrecognized—that keep unchurched people from attending and joining their cause.

The worship wars are over in growing churches. Most of the churches I've visited have a blended, contemporary style of worship that attracts and retains people. Some of them provide alternative worship experiences as a way of reaching a niche or affinity group who prefer something other than the primary worship service. In my visits to growing churches I've deliberately sought out some of their senior members to ask how they've adjusted to new worship styles and innovative programs. For the most part they are candid enough to admit that change is difficult but that it's worth giving up preferences to reach new people.

Growth occurs when congregations are convinced that their target audience is the unchurched public on the outside. They know that their own vitality is dependent upon turning the church inside out, giving up their preferences, and making the accommodations necessary to reach and retain new people.

The target audience is usually more specific than just the general unchurched public. For Pastor Jerry Moen at the Church on the Hill, the target audience is men between the ages of 25 and 40. He believes that if you can attract men, women and children will follow. He knows how they dress, the music they listen to, and what they'll respond to in church. Since many, if not most, men in the small western Oregon town where his church is located hunt and fish, the church sponsors an annual outdoor sports event that attracts more than 5,000 people to their campus, many of whom eventually visit and become involved in other church activities.

Some growing churches have identified several target audiences. The Grove City Church of the Nazarene provides a Saturday night worship experience for its extensive ministry to bikers. At the Spokane Valley church the Sunday evening service features traditional hymn singing and testimonies. The Trevecca Community church provides transportation for people in halfway houses and leads a worship service at a local jail on Sunday evening.

Immigrants are the target audience for many churches. Much of the United States and Canada will soon be majority-minority States like Hawaii, New Mexico, and California. Churches are adapting to these changes in some very innovative ways. I met with a group of pastors in the San Francisco Bay area each with a variation of what they call "one church with many congregations." This is more than providing a place for different autonomous congregations to meet in one church building. These churches reflect the multicultural society forming in California where people who may be identified by their cultural differences are at the same time constantly interacting with one another. These pastors provide culture-specific worship and social activities and recruit and train leaders from within these groups while involving them in a faith community that looks like the multicultural world around them.

Some of the fastest-growing churches in the United States are among the immigrant people groups, particularly Hispanics, Haitians, Koreans, and people from Caribbean countries. While not intentionally exclusive, their appeal or target audience is their own cultural community. In their own churches African-Americans are free to worship as they choose without having to accommodate to the majority culture. Many people groups often find that the best place to enjoy their own culture is in church.

The Brooklyn Beulah church is the fastest-growing and now

largest Black Nazarene congregation. The congregation, which appeals primarily to people from Caribbean countries, mostly from Barbados, has doubled in size to over 1,000 in attendance during the past eight years under the leadership of Pastor Wenton Fyne, a Jamaican immigrant. While the church now includes the American-born children and grandchildren of immigrant forebears, it has retained its identity as a haven for the Caribbean Diaspora in New York City.

African-American Pastor Dorzell King started one of the fastest-growing new churches in the greater Kansas City area. The Risen Lamb International Church of the Nazarene is unusual for its balance of African-American, white, and Hispanic members and friends. Since Pastor King's marriage is mixed, the congregation has become a place of refuge for many mixed-marriage families who are accepted without questions or uncomfortable stares. Risen Lamb's target audience is people who want a multicultural community, who don't want to go to church where everyone looks and sounds alike.

The Miami Bethany Church of the Nazarene with over 1,000 men, women, youth, and children in discipleship cell groups is one of the fastest-growing Spanish-speaking congregations in the United States. In 1995, Cuban immigrants, Pastors Obed and Noemi Jauregui, began their ministry with less than 50 members in a poor neighborhood three miles from the Miami International Airport. They have intentionally targeted immigrants from the Caribbean and Central America with a wide range of compassionate ministries, including emergency food and clothing.

After visitors from Mexico and Central America began attending the Grace Pointe Church in Indianapolis, they decided to target the growing Spanish-speaking immigrant community in their neighborhood. Under the long-term leadership of Pastor Keith Robinson, Grace Pointe has recently reinvented itself. This older, traditional congregation has taken on a new name in a new location. They've become intentionally multicultural and during the process have doubled their attendance. Spanish lyrics now appear on the screens along with English words as the congregation alternates between English and Spanish singing. Wireless headsets providing Spanish translation are offered to those who don't speak English.

Understanding the culture of a target audience is as much a missional challenge in the United States and other Western societies as it is any place in the world. Learning how to cross barriers of culture, language, and belief to communicate the good news of the gospel is the heart of missionary work. Churches in secularized, multicultural America know that these same missionary strategies are needed if they are to remain vibrant and growing.

The Salem Fields Community Church in Fredericksburg, Virginia, is expanding by adding new worship venues. Salem Fields has grown from 50 to over 1,500 in attendance under the husband-and-wife copastor team of Buddy and Gaye Marston. They now have a full-time staff member in charge of venue development who creates new worship experiences for affinity groups both on and off their main campus. Their new worship venues are designed to reach unchurched subgroups that are not necessarily defined by cultural or language differences.

Pastor Ron Salsbury has added a country-and-western weekend worship experience at the Pismo Beach, California, Community Church. Pastor Gene Tanner provides Thursday night worship for students at Valparaiso University designed around their interest in ancient symbols, liturgies, and a confessional fellowship. Pastor Craig Coulter knows that many of the new people in his rapidly growing Oro Valley, Arizona, congregation come from traditions accustomed to receiving Communion every Sunday. Rather than starting another service, he provides Communion at a table on one side of the sanctuary while others are kneeling at the altar at the front during the worship prayer time.

The Stillmeadow church in York, Pennsylvania—which has more than doubled in attendance during the past 15 years with Pastor Bud Reedy—provides a Saturday night service for people who are unlikely or unable to attend church on Sunday. The Saturday night services I've attended there and other places have a very different look and feel than Sunday worship. An intermission with refreshments was part of the Saturday night service at Stillmeadow—something they wouldn't do in their Sunday morning services.

Growing churches are missional. They've given up their preferences, discarded comfortable but ineffective routines, and have agreed that the church exists for its nonmembers. They embrace as well as challenge the secular cultures of unchurched people to effectively advance God's mission in the world.

II. PROFILES AND CONVERSATIONS

Albert Einstein claimed "imagination is more important than knowledge"; that may be as true for church development as it is for theoretical physics. There is no lack of information or knowledge about growing churches these days. Megachurches are everywhere with their highway billboards, engaging Web sites, and celebrity pastors. Books and consultants by the dozens tell the stories of how they have done it. Nevertheless, the majority of churches in the United States and Canada continue to plateau if not decline; it is not for lack of knowledge.

The following 11 profiles and conversations are not intended as how-to guides for building growing churches. They are meant to encourage the imagination. The pastors interviewed have innovatively adapted their training and life experiences to their own situations. They know you cannot grow a church by simply copying what others are doing. They learn from one another and pay attention to the trends in popular culture, including the church world. These stories have been selected from hundreds of growing churches where pastors have found ways of leading mission growth in spite of a culture that is in many ways hostile to church development. Good stories like these have been selected to encourage others to imagine what might be possible or, better yet, impossible in their own setting.

There are many right ways to grow a church. These best practices are just a few of the places where pastors are giving imaginative leadership to new mission growth movements. These pastors and others like them are impossibility thinkers who believe that with God's help the impossible is possible.

A Church Men Love to Attend

The Church on the Hill
McMinnville, Oregon
Jerry Moen, Pastor

Profile

It was the big Saturday at the Church on the Hill in McMinnville, a small town of 25,000, 50 miles southwest of Portland, Oregon. Thousands of people were on the church campus to attend the annual Sportsman's Show. Pastor Jerry Moen had invited me to experience the most important community outreach weekend of the year.

Jerry may be one of the most unlikely persons to be a pastor, let alone the pastor of a rapidly growing congregation. His father was an atheist, and although his mother was a devout Catholic who kept him in church, at age 11 he was given the choice to be confirmed in the Catholic faith or quit the church and stay at home with his dad. He remembers thinking this was the happiest day of his life, saying to himself, "I'm never going to have to go to church again. I'm going to stay home with Dad, and that will be great."

However, at age 16 his life took a dramatic turn. He followed his girlfriend to a Nazarene church where he eventually encountered God through a life-changing conversion experience. Although he had his sights set on becoming a game warden, the pastor told him he was going to be a pastor. Jerry can tell you the time and place, when and where he was saved, sanctified, and heard the "audible voice of God" saying, "You have given Me everything but your occupation, and that's what I want."

At the encouragement of that pastor, he attended Point Loma

Nazarene University to prepare for the ministry. After graduation in 1980 he served in a series of youth ministry assignments until 1992, when discouraged and exhausted he quit youth ministry. As he tells it, "I had some kind of burnout or meltdown."

He describes what happened. "I did ministry in my own strength. I was acting more like I was the savior instead of pointing people to the Savior." He admits he put the church before his family. His wife would tell him, "Jerry, the church is more important than your family," and he would deny this, saying, "No way, I preach that the family comes first." Then she would say, "Yes, but you don't live it." So he left the ministry to save his family as well as his faith.

They moved to McMinnville, Oregon, a small town about an hour's drive southwest of Portland, where he bought a farm and began working for his father-in-law as a landscaper and started attending the local Nazarene church.

Recognizing Jerry's faith and gifts, the pastor invited him to a part-time staff position that soon evolved into a full-time assignment in 1994. By then he was a different man. When he agreed to reenter full-time ministry, he decided he would never work more than five days a week. As he described it, "I did not want to have a savior complex, but instead, I wanted to really trust God that He could take care of His people without me there managing all the decisions and crises in their lives."

When the pastor resigned in 1999, Jerry was invited to become the senior pastor of this strong congregation of 600 situated in a good building set on a hill overlooking the valley. Since then the congregation has more than doubled in attendance. It is now known simply as the Church on the Hill, a place where men—especially men—and families crowd in for four weekend services, beginning on Saturday evening. In addition to the annual Sportsman's Show, which attracts several thousand to the campus, lay leaders sponsor a variety of outreach programs, including several hundred people in a wide variety of recovery groups.

In each of the four services the weekend I attended, the five individuals who had come to faith in Christ during the past week were introduced with their names on the screens. They were welcomed into the church family with applause and cheers. Pastor Moen described how they had come to faith and who had led them. A large lighted candle on the altar was the sign that someone had found their way to Christ and the church since they last met.

That Sunday Pastor Moen announced his plan to take a six-week sabbatical. He told the congregation, "I'm a little tired. I need a break. I'll return in six weeks renewed and ready to serve better." In each of the four services they clapped and shouted their approval and support.

Conversation with Pastor Jerry Moen

Tell me something about the mission of the church in the last six years. Who are you reaching?

We're located in a conservative, blue-collar county. The steel mill is our number one employer, agriculture is huge here in the Willamette Valley, and there's lots of logging in the coastal mountains. So we're very much a blue-collar community, and that's who we are reaching. We are reaching folks that have their kids in soccer, as well as folks who have their kids in foster care because of their drug and alcohol problems. We have a big ministry to the recovery community, with close to 300 people in our congregation who during the last five years have come out of the drug and alcohol world and entered a life of sobriety.

When you became senior pastor, wasn't the church already well established with a nice sanctuary?

Well, yes. This church started in 1911 and has a very rich heritage.

Somebody had foresight and vision, and a group of 200 people built this sanctuary, which seats close to 800 now. But by the time I got here in 1994, it felt churchy. I mean, we sang hymns with some choruses, but people dressed in suits and ties. And people acted just a little bit stiff. It was almost as if the church experience didn't quite fit real life. We had an orchestra and a choir. And it was just very, as we would say, churchy, which works great for people who like church, but when I became senior pastor, I just had this burning in my heart that said, "We've got to make what we do here appealing to people who don't like church."

At least church as they've known it, right?

Yes, church as they've known it. And so we got rid of the ties. Eventually the orchestra and the choir were just an occasional thing. Now the musical style is no different from what you would hear on your radio or in a store downtown. The lyrics are very different, because it's all contemporary Christian rock—except in the eight o'clock service where we sing hymns and some of the older choruses to help the people who really have a connection with this more traditional style.

How important is the sound of your music in worship to your growth and outreach to the target population?

When I became the senior pastor, we did two things simultaneously: we changed the dress climate, and we changed the music from what I call churchy to Christian rock and roll. We've got consistent quality with a good band, and we've gone from 600 to 1,200 in the last six years.

And you attribute that to the sound of the music?

I do, not to the music itself, but to the message it conveys.

But you have found that the sound in itself conveys a message apart from the words?

Yeah, it really does.

What's the message?

Well, that message is energy and passion. And, in fact, the second part of our five-part mission statement says that we will exalt God through passionate worship. And nobody ever comes here and accuses our music of being quiet or subdued or lacking passion. We want people to be passionate about everything in their Christian life, including the style in which they worship.

Who doesn't like it?

The folks who grew up on the hymns and the Gaither stuff. They don't like it. But I have not found people out in the community who don't like it. The lost people out there are attracted to the music.

And the dress code, how significant is that?

People come here and feel no one is putting on a show. This is especially important to folks who work at the steel mill or up in the woods logging all week long. If everybody is dressed up in suits and dresses, these folks look around and think the culture of this church doesn't match the culture of their community.

So you deliberately dress down?

Deliberately—absolutely! I fight with my wife every Sunday morning.

Why?

Well, she wants me dressed up, and she wants me to look nice. She tries to get me to dress so that I can somehow visually connect with the older generation—those who just feel they can hardly respect a pastor unless he's all dressed up. In contrast to them are the people in recovery who only own one pair of jeans and they wear them seven days a week. I have a natural tendency to want to dress down anyway. And my wife has a natural tendency to want to dress up, so it strikes a good balance.

During my visit I talked to several longtime members of the church, some of them were octogenarians. They were very excited about the church.

We have some of the greatest senior citizens of any church in the world. On Easter Sunday an 85-year-old member with tears in his eyes commented to me, "I don't recognize hardly anybody here, and I love that. You are reaching people that I have never met in my life."

I suppose you lost a few people, did you not?

Oh, there are several churches around here that received some great members from us. They just could not swallow the new music, and they thought I needed to preach more in-depth sermons on the weekends. There were also a few that left because we put ashtrays out in the parking lot. So, yes, we've lost some people. But the people that left here are on their way to heaven, and the people we gained were not.

Is the transition over?

I'm not sure we're through it yet. The first year I don't think I made too many waves. Most of the people stayed. I think it was probably my second year as senior pastor that we probably lost 40 or 50 people. These were good, old-time Nazarene folks who just said, "No, we can't do this." And it broke my heart, but those 40 or so left, and I think that year about 200 new people came.

Did you experience any financial challenge during the transition?

No. One year we had a 17 percent increase in giving over the year before. All the other five years have been 20 percent or higher over the giving of the previous year. This last year we experienced a 28 percent increase over giving the previous year.

And your attendance has increased about 100 each year since you became pastor.

Yes, I think it hit about 150 one year—but usually it's been about 100 people a year.

How do you make contact with new people?

We average 15 visiting families every Sunday, and those are just the ones that give us a card. When they come to the welcome center, they get a gift bag with a DVD about the church.

How do they find out about the church?

It's just word of mouth. That's all I can figure out. We don't pay for any regular advertising. There is an occasional event like a women's conference or a sportsman's show or a car club gathering, but we don't do any regular advertising. We're the largest church in our county, so it's just easy for folks to remember us. I'm involved in community things, and the Church on the Hill has people in virtually every business in town. It's pretty hard to have somebody out there who's not in contact with somebody from our church. I don't think our people can go through a service without hearing that they need to be reaching out to their friends and neighbors. So word of mouth brings them.

The Saturday Sportsman's Show I attended was a remarkable

experience. Several thousand neighborhood people were on your campus. How long have you been doing this?

This was our eighth year. The first year we probably had 500 people come. It's just growing to thousands and thousands of people that come every year now.

What is the reason behind all of the effort that it takes to organize that event?

All the leaders of our church agree that the target person we are going after is a man between the ages of 25 and 45.

Why?

Because we believe that if you get the man, you get the whole family. There are far too many women who come to church alone; their husbands just don't come. You know, there're all kinds of reasons why. David Murrow's *Why Men Hate Church* was a book that our entire staff and board and all lay leaders read. And it helped us realize that we have to be intentional to make the church a place where masculinity can be expressed. The natural tendency is to feminize church. You know, singing is much more preferred by women than it is by men. Look at the average choir, and it's 75 percent females and 25 percent males. And yet churches do a lot of singing. It's not necessarily a male-oriented activity.

And so the sportsman's event is unapologetically addressed to men, although there are lots of women and kids there?

Oh, yeah, we want the women and kids to come. It fits the culture of the county. Every weekend I'm going to refer to either hunting or football or classic cars. I'm going to use examples and illustrations that men can connect with. And because I've done that, the women of the church have unanimously thanked me for creating a church where their husbands want to come. When we target a man, we better have something in place that will minister to his children and his teens or he's not going to stay. Men are drawn to machines, to noise, to electric guitars.

Tell me about your small groups.

We have about 55 different small groups right now. We are averaging close to 500 adults in a weekly Bible study. That's over 50 percent. Right now we're averaging about 1,100 people in weekend worship.

Are you satisfied with that percentage?

No, I'm not. Our goal is to have 80 percent of our adults in a small group. So we haven't stopped doing Sunday School, but our small groups in homes are more than twice as popular as Sunday School.

If you add Sunday School to your small groups, you're up above 50 percent.

Oh, yeah, we're probably closer to 70 percent, but it would be a bookkeeping nightmare to try and figure out.

Apart from counting, why wouldn't you call a Sunday School class a small group?

Well, we do, but we just don't count them with the small groups because we don't want to double-count people. We also have small groups that are adult Bible classes. Those happen on Sunday mornings and Wednesday nights and are primarily educational settings with a little bit of fellowship thrown in as opposed to a home group where there is a balance between fellowship and prayer and Bible study.

What is the primary attraction to the Church on a Hill?

Over 80 percent of all the people that are in our church tell us that the first exposure they had was a Sunday morning service. Twenty percent or so come in through a special event or a home group or something like that.

What are people looking for?

I think they're coming because there's this buzz that has been created around town or around their store where they work, and they just want to see what's going on and I think they're looking for an encounter with God. Surveys tell us that people in the Northwest do care about spiritual things, and I think they are looking for answers to life's problems. They don't want to just hear Jesus is the answer. They've got to have more evidence than that.

What's an encounter with God?

I think part of it starts when they see a thousand people around them singing from their heart and just enjoying being together; and they have to look at that and say, "Wow, I have to get wasted to act like that, but these people are here just thoroughly enjoying one another and seemingly enjoying the presence of God." So I think that piques their interest right off the bat.

How do you describe your preaching?

I don't use the word *preaching*. People accuse me of not being a preacher and not really being a teacher. I sit on a stool. I use a music stand. It's extemporaneous—I use an outline for the sake of the PowerPoint people—but I'm just trying to have a conversation with 1,000 people all at the same time, trying to make it feel like a one-on-one discussion about things that matter in their lives.

What is your appeal? What do you bring to their encounter with God that is unique?

I think it is just such a relaxed approach.

You're obviously well prepared.

I spend eight hours on Monday and four hours on Wednesday on my message, but I'm trying to make it look like anybody out there can have the same kind of walk with God that I have. I don't want them to think you've got to be superspiritual or have some divine call on your life to be this passionate about your love for Christ. It needs to be attainable for everybody. I actually had a pastor once tell me, "Make sure that you always keep a distance between you and the people so they feel like you are closer to God than they are." And you know, I kind of understand that priestly role, but I don't want anybody in this town or in this church to think that I am in a spiritual position that they themselves could not obtain. And that just comes across. People just say, "Jerry, you connect with me." And I think I just lead them into a confidence that they are going to get where they want to be with Christ.

What do you see for the future? How long do you want to stay in McMinnville?

I'm going to stay in McMinnville all of my earthly life. They might not always want me as their senior pastor. Then I'll become a head usher or something. I'd love to be head usher. Someday that'll be my job.

What's the future for the church?

We're going to have to birth some new congregations, some new preaching points, some satellite campuses, something of that nature. We'll fill up our building four or five times a weekend, and we'll be able to reach 2,000 people and hold them here in this congregation while we also do our outreach program. There are some little towns around here that don't have Holiness churches. We just need to create some more preaching points out there. So I'm guessing 10 years from now instead of reaching 1,100 a weekend, we should be reaching 3,000 or 4,000 with a couple of other satellite locations and maximizing this place here.

Church as Theater

First Church of the Nazarene
Valparaiso, Indiana
Gene Tanner, Pastor

Profile

Valpo, as Pastor Gene Tanner calls it, looks like a traditional church in a small Indiana town. But what goes on here—that is, on what is called the Glendale campus—is anything but traditional. A renovated warehouse two miles away provides another campus for seven-day-a-week youth ministries as well as for the Common Ground and The Stain congregations. The worship experiences in both locations are sometimes referred to as venues. A staff member is assigned to venue development—designing new, innovative worship experiences for unreached target or niche groups.

When Pastor Gene Tanner began his ministry here in 1993, he immediately began to lead it from a plateaued church averaging 500 in attendance to what he calls a progressive church, which has been growing by 100 people annually for the last four years. The combined average Sunday worship attendance of the two services on each campus has exceeded 1,300 since the beginning of 2005.

On a recent Sunday morning I sat near the front for the first service at the Glendale campus. I couldn't help but notice how attentive the teens and children in front of me were. This wasn't a boring service for even the kids.

The stage, obviously renovated from a traditional platform, with the piano, organ, and pulpit removed, included a place for a band on the left, risers near the back for the choir, and two large overhead screens for announcements, video clips, and lyrics for singing. To the right were props for a dramatic presentation.

The houselights lowered as we began. Spotlights and background lighting changed constantly as the service moved from the band to the choir, from video clips to drama. And in the middle of the service, Pastor Tanner delivered his sermon from a center-stage mic. I was informed afterward that the woman with a clipboard and headset pacing in front of the stage was giving instructions to the sound and light control booths in the back. During the service there were at least 20 light changes.

As relaxed and informal as it felt, the service I attended was clearly choreographed, which was typical of what pastor Tanner describes as a concept service. Planning for each service begins months in advance with a sermon topic. The music, drama, video, and dance components are developed around an agreed upon concept. Stage sets and props are designed by the worship planning team and constructed by a group of volunteers in a building adjacent to the church. The worship team spends three hours or more rehearsing for each Sunday experience.

Following the first service at the Glendale campus I hurried away to the second service at the Common Ground campus. In an industrial part of town we parked in front of a single-story warehouse. This building is now used every day for youth ministries and on Sundays for worship experiences that attract people who Pastor Tanner says are not comfortable in a typical church setting.

After being served my free latte and biscotti in the front lounge, I entered the dimly lit worship area and took a seat with others around one of the tables near the stage. The pre-Easter season service concept was "CSI-Jerusalem." Having never seen the *CSI* (Crime Scene Investigation) TV program, I needed an explanation. The band, speaker, and ushers wore hats and T-shirts with the *CSI* insignia. If the music at the Glendale campus was soft rock, the music here was hard rock—a loud, throbbing sound, with video images in a darkened room and food for everyone.

Judging by the looks of the people and conversations around the tables, I had to agree that this was a worship experience designed for people who don't like church. But they liked this.

Conversation with Pastor Gene Tanner

When were you called to preach?

I was called late in life. I studied to become a speech pathologist—which seems strange because I'm a stutterer. While working for a hospital and a school system, I was helping in a Nazarene church in Port Huron, Michigan, and it began to hit me that I really loved what I was doing with the church and dreaded going to work. My uncle pastored that church, and one time he said, "You know you're called to ministry." I went to Olivet Nazarene University and explained that I had a degree and didn't particularly want to be a freshman but that I felt a call to ministry. They allowed me to graduate after completing courses in religion and theology. I did that in a year and then got my masters. I was a youth pastor for a couple of years, and then I went to a little church in Oxford, Ohio—I was off and running and never looked back.

How do you describe the Valparaiso church?

It's a bit unique—a larger church not in a large community. Valpo is a great community surrounded by corn. It's a town of 26,000—we do draw people from out of the community, but they must drive to us on purpose.

I have been here for the last 12 years. The church was started in 1924, and the present property was developed in 1980. The sanctuary seats 550 and was built specifically for a piano and organ. The building was not designed for what we've evolved to.

The church has experienced significant growth recently. How has that happened?

When I came, I knew we couldn't keep doing what we were doing. What we were doing was very old, very traditional—extremely traditional. In evaluating the culture of Valparaiso I felt our service style needed to change to become more relevant. I tried to change some very, very small things.

Oddly enough, we never failed to grow. The church has never plateaued. During the last 12 years the church has shown some increase every year. When two people would leave because of the change, three or four would walk in—so the walk-ins outnumbered the people leaving.

The problem was that the people who left were tithers—the people who walked in had not grown to that level yet. We grew every year, but there were a couple of years in the middle where we struggled financially. As discipleship took place, the finances began to rebound.

In the last 3 years we've grown by 100 a year. The first year we came, we averaged 448. We're halfway through this year and we have no Sundays under 1,100.

How did the church transition from a traditional church to what it is now?

We had to go from a cruise ship to a battleship. A cruise ship is where you are pampered and fed; a battleship is where everybody has a job to do. A lot of our churches are dying because they're great cruise ships—people just go to get pampered and fed.

We had to implement strategies to allow people ownership and get them involved in ministries. We began to put the team together—volunteers and paid staff.

What do you mean by worship venues?

Venues are the congregations that meet at our two sites. For instance, on Sunday the Common Ground site has two congregations. One meets at 9 A.M. and the other at 10:30. Those are two very different congregations.

In addition we have The Stain—which meets on Thursday nights. It's very experiential.

The Stain?

Yes, from stained-glass windows. The post high school group coordinates their own worship. They go from table to table; there's a devotional; and there's a table where you can take Communion by yourself. The beauty of this is that the service offers so many choices. There's also a table where you can light a candle and pray. This emerging culture is very much into symbols.

The service begins at 9 P.M. and ends at 10:00, but they hang out until about midnight. Here is something we realized—Barnes and Noble doesn't sell books, they sell an experience. Starbucks doesn't sell coffee but choices. The Stain is an experience with great choices.

What kind of experience?

We're discovering that the culture coming up—the collegiate culture—really wants hands-on experience. They don't want to be talked to. They want symbols—so we took stain from stained-glass window, which is a great symbol. There's a gigantic slide when you come in of a stained-glass window; it says, "Welcome to The Stain."

There are about seven tables of activities in The Stain. For instance, there is a confessional table where participants can write down their sins, and there is a shredder. There's a table where they can draw their emotions on big easels. The generation coming up wants their worship to be something they participate in. These tables allow individuals to express themselves through the arts, journaling, meditation, prayer, and the sacraments.

What is the Common Ground venue like?

Common Ground is extremely cutting-edge; it's edgy, contemporary, and takes everything a step farther. Common Ground is designed to create worship events that may not work at the main campus. Common Ground targets people with no church experience or a previous bad church experience.

In what way?

Here at the main campus we're going to push the envelope, but at Common Ground they're going to tear the envelope up. They write and design their skits. Right now they're doing a whole series based on rock music. There's a song by Avril Lavigne, "My Happy Ending," that the band comes in and does at about 100 decibels; it's geared for people who don't go to church, for people who are curious but are never going to walk into a church building. With Common Ground providing this ministry, we have become a single church ministering to three markets through three venues: Common Ground, The Stain, and the main campus.

You talked about concept worship at the Glendale campus. What does that mean?

Concept worship is the most difficult worship to do—but the most effective. It is difficult for the pastor because I must write way in advance. Right now at the end of October we're designing for February. We have a team of people who meet on Tuesday nights—they're extremely creative. I talk about where I would like to go—the thoughts I have—and they begin to build and design that service around that one teaching concept using music, drama, and props.

We have a building that's for constructing platform sets and storage because we use different sets all the time. Every Sunday the goal of concept is for people to walk out to the parking lot and have a buzz about the unbelievable experience they just went through.

No two services are exactly the same. They're built around the concept I want to teach. In order to do it well you must plan months in advance. The team will design it and then piece by piece put it together. Every week is huge. Wednesday night we rehearse— it's almost like putting a Christmas cantata on every week. Rehearsal usually goes from 6:30 to 9:30. There's drama and lighting, with usually 30 to 40 light cues per service.

When people come in, they come into a worship experience. They never know exactly what's going to happen, but they know it's going to be an experience that they can bring a friend to. It's almost as if you're walking into a theatrical experience every week.

Do people bring their friends?

Yes—that's why we're growing.

Is most of your growth from word of mouth?

All of it. We don't have a marketing budget.

You don't advertise?

Why? I have 1,300 agents—1,300 people who are telling somebody else about their church. They talk about what happened Sunday. And people get curious and they want to come and find out what we're going to do this week.

I read a statement in a marketing magazine. It was about Howard Stern. People listen to his show not because they like him but because they want to see what he's going to do next. That hit me. There are people who come to our church who haven't found Christ yet, but they're going to; we call them pre-Christians, not the lost. We believe in them enough that we call them pre-Christians. They come here because they want to see what we're going to do this week.

How do all these new people connect with one another?

We buy into the Saddleback philosophy. We've taken their program and *Wesleyaned* it up a bit. That is huge. Last year we took in over 115 members from the 101 class. Once you complete 101, you can apply for membership. I teach the class; it's five hours over two weeks.

We make sure they understand that we're a church with six services or congregations. If you want to be anonymous, you can be—but we don't want you to be. We are prepared right now as you come out of 101 to put you in a small group.

What percentage of your people are in small groups?

Not as many as I'd like—35 to 40 percent. It has to be for those who are new. The people who've been here forever don't need small groups; they already have their circle of friends.

How do small groups and adult Sunday School interact?

They're one and the same. We don't have enough Sunday School classrooms. We have small groups meeting in restaurants, homes—you name it. They get curriculum. We have some small groups that are not Sunday School. We have guys that hunt—they're a small group. But most small groups are involved in some type of ministry or study. All the staff are in small groups. My small group is going through Blackaby's book *Experiencing God.* Any small group can go through any book they want as long as we approve it.

Most of the Sunday morning Sunday School is for children and teens. A few adult groups meet then but not many.

What do you wish you could improve?

I wish I had 75 percent of my church in small groups. There are lots of people who choose not to be in a small group. I think part of the reason is that they're overcommitted. They see it as just one more thing to do.

How do you follow up on visitors?

Every Sunday there are visitors. They fill out a card if they feel comfortable. I go to their home—I personally call on every visitor. I get to meet them, ask them why they came. I'm always curious why somebody walks into a church. We haven't solved how to assimilate these people quickly. It's not how to get people to come—our biggest battle is how to assimilate people walking in. We're gaining a hundred a year. If we could find a way to assimilate faster, we could go to a 150 to 200 increase a year.

How do you integrate the Holiness message in your preaching?

We are very aggressive on discipleship. We tell our church that we are growing—growing quickly—so wouldn't it be a crime to wake up five years from now and realize that we're 10 miles wide and an inch deep.

What does that mean?

It means we must totally give ourselves to Christ, that Christ has our all in all. There must be a way that we can open ourselves up so much that the Holy Spirit totally dominates our lives. We talk about what it says in Acts when Paul asked the new believers whether they had received the Holy Spirit. I ask that same question to those who have come to Christ. "Have you been filled, possessed—where you lay down everything before Christ and say, 'I am Your disciple'?" And then we add, "It's not about making this church strong; it's about making sure you don't miss any blessing God has for you." Everything is in the positive.

Is your denominational connection a value added to your outreach?

Yes—predominantly in missions. A lot of people come from independent churches. We never make an excuse for saying the sign in the front of the building reads Church of the Nazarene. I tell them that we can do more as a whole than we can as individual churches. So we're in 150 world areas—that's huge—the Valparaiso church is in 150 world areas with over 700 missionaries. We always come back to the fact that we're part of this whole and that we can do more plugged in globally to the whole than we could if we were just by ourselves.

How many of your members are new to the Church of the Nazarene?

One hundred a year. The negative part of that is when I hear from people who move and are on the lookout for a Valparaiso Nazarene Church in another city and I have to tell them every church has the privilege to design themselves to be culturally relevant where they are. We're unique. Every Nazarene church has the privilege of being unique.

What is your worship music and your worship experience like at the Glendale campus?

Soft rock—edgy. We still use the choir, but we don't do typical choir numbers. And we don't use the choir every week. We sometime use hymns, but this is rare and they're typically redesigned. We don't have a pulpit; we use a music stand. It's seeker-sensitive. For people that don't know about church, seeing a guy behind a pulpit is a negative image. We've done a lot of research about people who don't go to church and what turns them off when they walk in. One of the things is the pulpit. It's not life and death to us—we're not worshiping the pulpit.

You've got to find a way to engage the crowd in this kind of service so that when you're preaching, they don't know it. Like, we're all just relaxing in the living room and talking about something. If they get the sense you're preaching, you're done.

What advice do you have for pastors looking toward leading a church through transition?

Move an inch at a time, realizing that every time you move, someone is going to leave. There are many "that was the last straw" kind of people. If you move the church all at once and lose them all at once, you can't absorb it. You move it real slow, and before you move it, make sure you have enough credibility to move it.

A Resurrection Church

First Church of the Nazarene
Harrisonburg, Virginia
Kerry Willis, Pastor

Profile

At the close of each of the three worship services I attended on a recent Sunday morning at the Harrisonburg First Church of the Nazarene, Pastor Kerry Willis encouraged the people to come forward and place a "Connection Collection" in a basket at the front of the auditorium. He repeated one of his favorite appeals: "No pressure, just pleasure." The offering was for three pressing needs beyond local church expenses: (1) to help an elderly couple purchase unaffordable medicine, (2) to pay the transportation and food expense for a picnic hosted by Nazarenes for their Muslim neighbors in Jordan, and (3) to support one of their church members on a year-long volunteer mission in Germany.

Since so many people came forward to welcome the new members received in each service—over 30 total—it was hard to tell how many of the 1,400 in attendance had contributed. When it was added up, more than $8,000 was given to this unannounced offering—above their tithe giving and additional offerings for missions.

The generosity of that spontaneous offering tells the story. This is a church with a global as well as local mission, responding to the needs of its neighbors even as it find ways to help people a world away.

Since its relocation in 1999 to the present 16-acre campus on the edge of Harrisonburg, Virginia, in the heart of the Shenandoah Valley, the church has grown by an average of 200 each year.

The Harrisonburg story is really about Kerry Willis. After his marriage to Kim in 1980, the young couple moved from North Carolina to Harrisonburg to pursue a career opportunity in studio photography. At the urging of his mother they agreed to visit the local Church of the Nazarene. Although they were strangers to the denomination as well as the congregation, they were warmly received and came to faith. Kerry and Kim eventually left the East Coast and his photography business and moved to Colorado Springs to attend Nazarene Bible College.

While there Kerry learned that the Harrisonburg church had fallen upon hard times. He let it be known that if the opportunity ever came, he would love to be the pastor of the church that led him and his wife to faith. That opportunity came in 1994 when at the invitation of the congregation he left school and moved back to Harrisonburg to become pastor of a discouraged and divided congregation of 120 people.

GROW Magazine once described Harrisonburg First Nazarene as a "resurrection church"—a declining congregation that might not have survived had it not been for the dramatic turnaround under the leadership of Kerry Willis. Now with their membership over 1,000, attendance approaching 1,500, and a preschool with 175, the church is served by a pastoral staff of 9, with Kerry as the Vision Pastor. There are an additional 10 on the administrative staff and over 20 employees of the preschool. The church budget is now over $2.5 million. In 1996 Kerry Willis was named pastor of the year for the region by Eastern Nazarene College.

Harrisonburg First Nazarene is an example of a growing number of churches with direct global mission programs. Even as these churches support denominational mission programs, they have become mission agencies themselves, engaged in direct, point-to-point giving and partnerships.

Kerry has taken members of his staff and congregation on three trips to the Middle East to encourage pastors in Jordan and Nazareth, including pastors preparing to start churches in Iraq. At the invitation of Rod Green, missionary to Jordan, Kerry and his people have been asked to do more than give money. Rod asked them to come to Jordan to get acquainted with Arab Nazarenes. Making the journey to bring encouragement and support would mean more than giving dollars. Kerry is now planning to visit Northern Iraq as preparation for later mission excursions by members of the congregation.

Conversation with Pastor Kerry Willis

What did you find when you came to the church in 1994?

When the district superintendent called to invite me to consider coming to Harrisonburg, he said, "Kerry, I need to tell you they're in a fight over there." The board and the people were meeting each other head on. But when I came, it was as though one of their boys had come home. They all loved me because I wasn't there when the trouble started. There had been a mass exodus of people. I went and visited many of them, and I asked them to come back—and they did. The Sunday before I came, there were 121 people. In 1994 they averaged 150. We went to 200 real quick.

When did things begin to change?

I came in and preached encouragement. I called my mother and asked, "If I were your pastor, what would be one piece of advice you'd give me?" She said, "Kerry, when you go to the pulpit, bring a word of encouragement." She said, "They've been beat up all week. Please don't take the baseball bat to your people." I took that literally. And then I preached 19 straight Wednesday nights on prayer. People were asking me, "Do you know anything else?" Our people began to be a praying church 20 weeks into the ministry.

Your Sunday sermon had a strong emphasis on unity, together-ness, being connected. Why is that?

I've emphasized that from day one. I'll tell you where I got it. In 1994 I read an article by Lyle Shaller in *Leadership Magazine.* It was the first thing on leadership I ever read. He wrote that you must make unity your vision. The Lord gave me the idea of focusing forward for future generations. The people had never seen a vision for the church. As you heard on Sunday, our vision is for the Shenandoah Valley, the state of Virginia, and beyond.

Why did you make plans for new property and larger buildings?

We decided we needed to relocate after we got to about 250 people. I called John Maxwell with the Injoy group about doing a capital campaign. We agreed to pay them about $30,000, and they were going to teach us how to do it. They just give you the tools, but you have to work it. That was a lay-led stewardship campaign. Our people pledged beyond the tithe and Faith Promise $550,000 over three years. From that campaign our people began to believe in generosity. One word describes the people here—*generosity!* That's the word. Every other week we take an offering that has nothing to do with us.

When did you relocate?

We moved out of the old building in 1997 and into the new one in 1999. We were meeting in a school for almost 2 years. While there we grew from 275 to 325. We purchased 16 acres and now we wish we would have bought more. After we bought this corner, a developer built homes on the 90 acres around us. This is one community from which we draw every Sunday.

You've gained about 1,000 in 6 years, right?

I used to think we would gain 1,000 in 10 years. Last Sunday we had over 1,400—but I'm not really focused on the numbers. Someone suggested that we do a Forty Days of Purpose program. I told them that we're engaged 365 days and I don't want that to change. I got a tape from Rick Warren in 1997; here's what I got from him: "You focus on health and you'll grow the church."

What is the magnet that draws people to your church?

Lots of different things, but this is the main thing. I heard H. B. London give a statistic—that if you win men to God, 94 percent will win their whole family to Christ. I've tried to make church relevant to men—a place where they would want to come. I took over men's ministries myself. The first thing I did was to have a men's retreat. I told the guys we'd take my dad's shrimp boat and go on a three-day fishing trip—and 19 men signed up. (I knew I wanted to come home to the North Carolina coast to go fishing, but I didn't have enough money to go.) The next year we had 25 and then 35. This past year we had 105! We have won men to God. The men in our church are not AWOL.

What's different about a church focused on men?

The big thing is we've designed ministry for men. I called a prayer team together—a men's prayer team. I started with 7 men. I recruited them. The next year I multiplied it. I preach a lot about life-saving stations. I use a lot of men's stories. I had 7 men praying when I started and now I have 70 signed up. I sign them up every year. I say, "It's not pressure, just pleasure." There are three things you have to do to be a part of this team. Number one, you have to pray. Number two, you must pray for Pastor Kerry at least one day a week. And number three, with God's help, you will pray with Pastor Kerry at least once a week.

What are some of the things the church has had to change in order to grow?

One thing—we canceled Sunday night. I told the people that this is going to bother you because it used to bother me. But if you keep doing the same thing you've always done and get the same old thing you've always had, you ought to look at it. I told the people we had two starving horses: one was called Wednesday night and one was called Sunday night. Neither one of them was well fed. We shot one of them—Sunday night—and gave his food to Wednesday night. And now it's no big deal to have 500 people on Wednesday night.

What do you do on Wednesday night?

Bible studies (I do lecture-style Bible studies), children and youth programs, and a ton of others things. I used to hear it said, "If you love the preacher, you'll come on Sunday night; if you love the church, you'll come on Sunday morning; if you love the Lord, you'll come on Wednesday night." I told the people from the pulpit, "I already know you love me, so Sunday night is not important." We put everything into Sunday morning, and instead of coming back and rewinding, we come back fresh Wednesday night. This change began while we were meeting in the school. Since we couldn't get the school Sunday night, we had to do everything on Sunday morning.

How did you break the 200 barrier?

At 250 we had to start thinking bigger. Thinking was the biggest barrier. Teaching and Sunday School have been the biggest challenge. We've had Sunday School all over the place. We used to have it on Sunday morning right before worship. Then when we grew and had to go to two services, we put Sunday School in the middle. It was all right, but our people were worn out. Then we went to Sunday night Sunday School and moved the services closer together. Now we have a lot of classes on Wednesday night. We try to teach in different venues. But teaching has been the biggest challenge.

Is this a staff-driven or board-driven church?

It's staff-driven with board approval. The board gives us the privi-

lege to go with it, and we report to them. The board provides ac-
countability for the staff. They want us to do the ministry because
they have full-time jobs. The way to get the best board is to get a
busy board.

How have you changed as the church has grown?

I had to become less in the church. If there is anything I would have
changed, I would have made it less about Kerry Willis. What I mean
is, here's my style—I overpromise and I overdeliver. When I took my
sabbatical after eight years, I realized that I have to get myself out of
that church so that it's not just one person. There have to be other
leaders at every level.

Any other changes?

I had to become more risky and less controlling. I'm a delegator, yet
I'm always available. My number's in the phone book. But I can go
all day and not get a call. To me that's success. I had to change my
schedule. I meet with individual staff members as needed on Mon-
days and the whole staff every other Thursday morning—I meet
them together and individually. Tuesday is my quiet day—my day to
pray, to be with the Lord. Wednesday is my sermon preparation day
at home and then I go to the church at 4 P.M. I do some counseling
from 4:00 to 7:00. I meet with anybody who calls me. I teach a Bible
study on Wednesday evening. People love that. Thursday I'm in the
church all day. I'm there to encourage the workers. Friday is my
wife's day. Unless it's an emergency, nobody sees me but her on Friday. Saturday is "do whatever needs to happen" day. Sunday I
preach my head off.

What is success in the ministry?

In a seminar 10 years ago I heard John Maxwell say, "Here's the true
measure of success. After 10 years you've almost worked yourself

out of a job. But the people keep you because they love you and need your inspiration."

How do you design your worship services?

We just changed everything around on Sunday mornings to give our Spanish-speaking venue a great slot for growth. As a result, we now have two English-speaking worship services, both blended in style. The first English-speaking service begins at 9 A.M., and the second is close on its heels at 10:15 A.M. Then immediately the live-wired Latino beat begins, as the Spanish-speaking venue—also in the main worship center—kicks off at 11:30 A.M. We have plans to begin a third English-speaking service on Saturday evenings in the fall of 2007 with a family-friendly worship feel. Also, a local businessman is trying to get clearance to build a country-Branson-style theater about 10 miles east of our location near a large, four-season mountain resort. Upon opening, he has asked us to provide a worship venue at the location on Sunday mornings. All in all, let me explain in a few sentences our newest approach to worship: We're working intricately to become a church that emphasizes simplicity so we can return the word *rest* to our Sabbath days and to all of our days. We're learning that one spelling for *hope* these days is *rest*. It's a Matt. 11:28-30 thing.

When did your mission to the Middle East begin?

I met Rod Green, a missionary to the Middle East, in 2000 on a tour of the Holy Land. There I was introduced to Nizar Touma, an Arab Nazarene pastor in Nazareth and Jerusalem. I had never met an Arab Christian. To me that was an oxymoron. I didn't understand that. He helped me understand my ignorance. He made a comment that Arab Christians wonder how Americans feel about them. Later, one Arab Nazarene pastor told me that he received a call from an American who wanted to bring a Work and Witness team to the

Holy Land, but when he found out they were an Arab congregation, he hung up. I determined to change that kind of thinking.

How has your mission partnership developed?

When Rod Green came to the States, I asked him what we could do to help. He didn't ask for a big offering. He said, "Please come. I need someone who can encourage pastors." I asked, "Where are you located?" He said, "Amman, Jordan." I never planned to go to Amman, Jordan. It didn't appeal to me. But I told him on the spot I'd go. I returned in 2004 to teach and preach to the Jordanian people who now included Iraqi pastors—among them, Aziz, who went back to Baghdad to start a church. In 2005 we took 15 on a Work and Witness team to Jordan.

What difference has this mission partnership in the Middle East made in the church?

Let me tell you a story. On the afternoon of 9/11, 2001, my phone rang. The answering machine came on. It was Nizar Touma—an Arab man with an Arab accent—and he was weeping as he prayed for our church and for our people. I played that recorded message on Sunday morning. I told the people that those men who flew the planes into our buildings do not represent Arab people. That's the kind of blessing we receive. When we tell people of our mission to the Middle East, it charges their passion for mission in our neighborhood.

What is your vision for the future of the Harrisonburg church?

I heard Leonard Sweet say you can have two kinds of churches, a church that makes a difference in the world or a church that makes the world different. I chose the second.

From 300 to 1,600 in 18 Years

Stillmeadow Church of the Nazarene
York, Pennsylvania
Bud Reedy, Pastor

Profile

In his 18 years as pastor at the Stillmeadow Church of the Nazarene in York, Pennsylvania, Bud Reedy has led the church from an average attendance of 300 to over 1,600. This remarkable record of steady, sustained growth is the result of change—a pastor who knows how to lead change and a congregation willing to change locations, worship style, organizational structure, and its target audience.

Reedy, a graduate in communication arts from Eastern Nazarene College (1975) and from Nazarene Theological Seminary (1980) confesses that he's more comfortable with a mic in his hand before a thousand people than in a one-on-one conversation. Nevertheless, he's delegated to others nearly all of the church administrative responsibilities so that he can be available to the guy who calls and says, "Hey, Pastor Bud, can we meet for breakfast? I just need to talk to you."

He came to the York, Pennsylvania, church in 1990 because, he says, the congregation was serious about making disciples. They were doing everything they knew to do to grow but were limited to the confines of their downtown location. In 1992 they moved to a 20-acre site in a then underdeveloped area north of town and soon the growth began even as the population increased around them.

They built a multipurpose building—a big rectangular structure that continues to serve as a gymnasium as well as a worship center for more than 600 people. Other buildings have been added since to provide seven-day-a-week programs for children and youth. They've grown the attendance by adding worship times on Friday and Saturday nights, organizing a Hispanic worship center in downtown York, and having multiple Sunday services on the main campus. Pastor Reedy describes Stillmeadow as "one church with many congregations."

Conversation with Pastor Bud Reedy

What kind of changes have come with your growth from 300 to over 1,600?

Once we clearly established our mission statement and identified our core values, then we began to organize ourselves around those core values. One of the things that we changed was the old program that worked for years—Sunday School at 9:30 A.M., worship at 11 A.M., a Sunday evening evangelistic service, a Wednesday night prayer meeting, revival meetings that brought people in every night, and people participating in leadership mostly by being on various boards. That traditional Wesleyan-Holiness congregational spiritual formation model was no longer working. That's because society had changed so quickly. People's schedules are so much more complex. You often have two working parents, so the church is no longer the center of the community's cultural life—the public school is. And so you have a church that was asking families for three to five time slots a week when those times were no longer available. So here's what we did—we decentralized everything. We have worship services at a variety of times. Our small groups are all over the map. Sometimes they're in people's homes; sometimes on the campus. Some are on Sunday night, some Wednesday night, and some Tuesday morning in a restaurant. We spread our small groups all over the place.

What percentage of your people are in small groups?

I've not done a survey recently, but probably 30 to 50 percent. I wish that were a better number. We do everything possible to make small-group participation accessible. We have a great variety of small groups. We have some traditional Christian education classes; we have a marriage and family track, a recovery track, and a ministry-oriented track. Our choir now is a small group because they have an approved teacher and curriculum with 30 minutes of Bible conversation. That's the only criteria for a small group. We try to make our small groups, our worship services, and our ministry opportunities more accessible to people. We made the transition. We no longer say, "Here's the church, here are the programs we offer at these specific times, and families, you need to adjust your lives to fit into the church's schedule." What we now say is, "Here are all the ministry options, small groups, youth and children's programs, and worship services we provide. You know your own family schedule, so you custom-fit what works based on your schedule and your needs." We take a menu approach—you can join this small group, attend this worship service, get involved in this ministry. We try to do this in such a way that it only requires people to give one or two time slot commitments a week to the church.

All this was a huge change for our people. I remember a board retreat in 1995 when I presented this concept. It was very, very difficult especially for those longtime Nazarenes who had been so thoroughly indoctrinated into the old traditional Wesleyan-Holiness congregational spiritual formation model. Those were some tough meetings. But I just kept returning to the notion that if we're really going to reach families, if we're really going to pull them into the center of our church's life, then these kinds of adjustments will be needed.

With all that variety, what holds the church together with a common identity?

Our mission statement and core values. We no longer say, "OK, if you're a good Nazarene and if you're a Spirit-filled Christian, you're going to be here Sunday morning, Sunday night, and Wednesday night; you're going to be here for 12 nights of revival; and you're going to be involved on three boards." What we say is, "Are you building these five core values into life—devotion, worship, discipleship, service, and witness? Here are the many different ways you can implement these things." We no longer ask, "Were you on the campus on Sunday night?" In fact, we don't even ask, "Were you on the campus Sunday?" because we have people who worship on Saturday night and on Friday night. So we just ask different questions. This is still a high-expectation, high-level-of-commitment church. We don't feel that that's been compromised at all. It's just that we've changed the way we talk about spiritual growth, spiritual formation, and Christlikeness.

As you've changed the church programs to meet the needs and schedules of those you're adding, what changes have you had to make in the organizational structure of the church? What internal changes have been necessary to drive this growth?

In 2002 we invited Bobby Huffaker, then the pastor at Grove City, as a growth consultant. Although our staffing and programs reflected our core values, our structure did not. We had the old traditional board structure, the one outlined in the Nazarene *Manual,* which is for a small to medium church model. The first thing Bobby said to us was that our church had outgrown its organizational structure. He made some recommendations that would make our organizational structure and decision-making processes represent our church's core values.

After implementing the changes Bobby recommended, there are now 18 people elected to the church board. Upon their election they are asked which of our four boards they want to serve on. We no longer have just one church board. We've organized our four boards around our core values. There's a worship board, a discipleship board, a service board, and a witness board. They meet 3 times a year. We also have a leadership gathering with all the boards 3 times a year. So the board members meet just 6 times a year instead of 12. That was the final stroke of the pen for Stillmeadow to become a staff-led church as opposed to a board-led church.

How did those changes result in a staff-led church?

We had an understanding that when you're elected as a board member, you are elected as a specialist to one of those four boards. One of our four core staff members chairs each of those boards. When we come together, we are there to pray and to set policies. It's the expectation of the church board that the pastoral staff is authorized and empowered to carry out those policies. So we don't have boards selecting the color of the paint in the hallways and determining what kind of toilet paper we're going to buy. The finance committee establishes our budget so that each of our four staff people understand what our budgets are. We have a job description for each of those boards, and when the boards all meet as one, we pray and we examine how we are carrying out our ministry—are we truly a values-driven church? Opinions are shared and policies are established.

Do you have nonelected board members serving on the boards?

Yes. For instance, on the discipleship board that Pastor Wayne Lynch chairs, there are both elected board members and appointed board members. People who are elected to our church boards must already be involved in some ministry in the church, whether teaching a small group, singing in the choir, or serving in some ministry in the trenches. We don't want folks sitting on boards who are disconnected from the service opportunities of our church.

What changes have you had to make in your personal leadership style?

We have 16 on our pastoral staff now, 9 of whom are part-time bivocational who have been hired from within. Those 9 people are involved in theological education by extension. These are people who have been saved and filled with the Holy Spirit at Stillmeadow and called to the ministry. They see Stillmeadow as a place where it's easy for people to say yes to the call of God upon their lives. Every time we add a staff person, everyone else's job description changes, including mine. I remember John Bradshaw—a popular psychologist back in the '80s—who said that a symbol for a family in balance is like a mobile that hangs over a crib; it's made up of animals or little planes hanging from strings, and when one of them moves, they all move and all adjust in some way—some higher, some lower, some to the left or to the right. That's my view of what must happen when you add or lose a staff member—everybody needs to adjust. In the 18 years I've been at Stillmeadow my job description has changed 18 times.

What are the most significant changes?

One significant change was when Wayne Lynch became our senior executive associate. He is now the director of the pastoral staff. He hires, fires, and reviews our pastoral staff performance. I am totally out of that loop. He consults with me, but that's basically his responsibility. Before Wayne did that, I was doing 20 pastoral staff reviews a year. I was determining who should get raises and who wouldn't. It's very, very difficult to be a pastor/mentor to the staff and also be their supervisor. So that has been a huge shift. Now I would like to think that my primary role with the pastoral staff is to bring them under my wing and nurture them and bring them along.

How many staff do you evaluate?

Just our two senior associates.

Since you can't spend time with everyone in a large, growing church, how do you manage your time?

I do not have a day off. I look at my calendar each month and I choose two three-day periods when I get out of town. Twice a month my wife, Sally, and I get away to the shore. We leave on a Sunday afternoon and come back on Wednesday.

On Tuesdays I meet with the pastoral staff—Wayne Lynch chairs that but I'm there to lead the devotional time. I'm there to encourage. Friday mornings I meet with the executive staff.

Most of my sermon preparation begins during two week-long time slots when I just get away and write sermons for the year. I preach almost exclusively sermons in series. Sally and I will get away, and I'll bring a bookcase full of books and write the outlines for 20 to 40 sermons.

On my regular schedule I'm in my office some, but my focus these days is on getting out and meeting with people over breakfast—just trying to do some spiritual direction with the people. I plan it as opportunities and needs arise. I want to keep my schedule just as clear as possible so that I can respond to the guy who calls me and says, "Hey, Pastor Bud, can we meet for breakfast? I just need to talk to you."

How involved are you with worship preparation?

Our public worship pastor has responsibility for the orders of worship, including media. He directs all of our worship services and will be the director of multiple public worship pastors at various sites. I don't know where it will end—maybe 10 to 20 worship sites. He wants the worship order done a month in advance.

Do the services build around your sermons?

They really don't. There are different schools of thought on this. There are some people who feel very strongly that worship services should be thematic. I was at Willow Creek last Sunday. There it is—a thematic worship service. Everything that occurred in that worship service was around the theme Pastor Apple has developed for that particular service. I'm not comfortable with that. They have one theme that they're driving home in a worship service. It's a strong possibility that you may be missing people. I like the idea of having hymns about the Second Coming and a prayer time with a different focus, with a sermon that's not necessarily directly connected theologically with the rest of the service.

What is distinctive about your worship experiences?

I work very hard on keeping a close connection between pulpit and altar. Our worship pastor has learned that he's got to give me enough time to not only preach the sermon but also draw in the net. We put a lot of emphasis on the response to the sermon. That reflects our Holiness tradition. For me—maybe I'm an old-fashioned guy—but for me there will always be a very close connection between altar and pulpit. I preach to the will, and I preach for decision. The worship pastor views the music as setting the table for the proclamation event.

Do you use video and drama?

Some. We have a part-time drama director, but we don't do a lot of the Willow Creek vignettes. We have big dramatic productions three or four times a year. I pull video into my sermons when I feel it's appropriate. I'm not a big PowerPoint guy—I'm not much for PowerPoint word presentations—I prefer images. He's always looking for creative ways to help people imagine what is being preached.

Your preaching is dramatic. You're not afraid of introducing dramatic presentations and themes. You use humor. What is your preaching style?

It is really narrative-driven. People are hardwired to receive stories. I love the narrative part of preaching. I do that with a dramatic flair. I was a communication arts major in college—I can't help myself.

You have stage presence. I've watched you—you're comfortable onstage.

I'm more comfortable with a microphone before a thousand people than I am one-on-one with people.

What draws people to worship at Stillmeadow?

There is an excitement and energy that you feel as you walk into the building. We just spent $100,000 turning our foyer into a welcome area with a coffee bar. When people walk through the door, we want the first seven minutes to be wow! We want to make raving fans out of them. When people have a good experience, we don't have to ask them to go tell somebody else. They're going to tell somebody else. We work very hard on the first seven minutes.

Seven minutes of what?

Finding a good parking place. Being warmly greeted with the information they need when they walk through the door. We don't want people wandering around trying to find the nursery. We want them to find the nurseries and the bathrooms quickly. When they walk into the worship center, they'll find a good seat near the end of the row where they won't have to crawl over people. Five minutes before the service begins there's a countdown video that puts everyone on alert—there's something exciting coming. The service begins with a bang. We like big-time praise music at the beginning. We work very hard—no matter what style of music, whether it's traditional, blended, or contemporary—at keeping the music uplifting, exciting, and joyful. We've come to the conclusion that most of the people who walk through our doors are consumers. I don't even like the way that sounds, but the last time I checked, this is a capitalistic society and our people have been indoctrinated to think and act and behave as consumers. Most of the people who walk through our doors know exactly what they're looking for in church.

Which is?

I would like to think that it's an exciting place to worship God—where the Word of God is proclaimed. It's a warm and inviting place where you're welcomed. Most people who walk through the doors are thinking, "If they don't have something for my kids, I'm out of here." One of the things we repeat over and over is, "Stillmeadow needs to be a place where kids are first." So we have three staff members in the children's division. We give them great space. The children's department hopefully is our strongest department.

The first seven minutes introduces people to a worship experience.

It's an attraction. I believe that Christian worship should be both fiesta and funeral. We have a time for grieving in the pastoral prayer time—a time for grieving our losses. It's not all this pie-in-the-sky-by-and-by stuff. I would like to think that we get real.

It's not boring or predictable.

We don't distribute an order of worship. Just the people who are leading worship have one. But we like people sitting on the edge of the seat, standing on tiptoe. I really like it that they just don't know what's coming. One of the reasons I want a full 45 minutes to preach is because spontaneous things often happen. It's sort of a planned spontaneity. We want to be sure we have plenty of room in that service for God to change the order of things. At the close of some of our services I just shake my head and tell myself I'm not smart enough to put something like this together. It's such a God thing. You must leave space for God. If everything is orchestrated and choreographed, we wouldn't have time if the Holy Spirit decided to move.

How do you keep up with trends and new ideas?

Ministry in the 21st century is changing so rapidly that it seems to me that the leading theologian of a church needs to make sure that he or she is blocking out plenty of time for reading and reflection. I've always got a book working, some stuff I'm wrestling with. Just recently I read a book by Thom Rainer called *Simple Church.* For me it was a confirmation of our emphasis on being values-driven and having a discipleship program that is sequential, easy to understand, and a process though which we are intentionally moving people. This was not so much a new idea as it was verification to me that we were striving to be a "simple church" and didn't even know it. The lead theologian and dreamer in a congregation has to be a person who is keeping his or her ear to the ground.

I know you are committed to cultural inclusion. You're working on a book on the subject. Why is that important to you?

Stillmeadow, like a lot of communities, is becoming more and more diverse. By the year 2020 the city of York will have no majority group. The largest group will be Hispanic. When I arrived here, 3 to 5 percent of the congregation were people of color. Now it's close to 12 percent. It's been an interest of mine because I feel that the church as a whole in the United States needs to address this issue because of the diversification of our world.

What will your book be about?

A discussion of the Great Commission—making disciples among all people groups—and some of the various models that churches are using to improve their multicultural ministry effectiveness. It's going to offer a curriculum that I hope local churches will use to improve their effectiveness in making disciples in the nations.

What advice do you have for pastors?

You don't have to convene a committee or to have a denominational commission to figure out what our mission is. Jesus made that abundantly clear. Our mission is to make disciples, more disciples, better disciples. That must remain true north for us as a denomination.

Do you have a word for denominational leaders?

I cannot begin to express how pleased I was with the announcement that our denominational mission statement is "To make Christlike disciples in the nations." That's who we are. I know down through the years there's been a strong emphasis on our denominational distinctive being entire sanctification as a second work of grace and, in the words of Bresee, to Christianize Christianity. I love the Church of the Nazarene and grew up in the Wesleyan-Holiness tradition. Doctrinally I am there. But I was so encouraged with Mike Lodahl and Tom Oord's book *Relational Holiness.* For me they have become the voice for many of us who feel very strongly that we have to find a way to articulate our Holiness doctrine that's consistent with our missional mandate. The mission statement from our denominational leaders and the book by two outstanding theologians were a tremendous encouragement to me that we are really asking the right questions and moving in the right direction.

You talk about God's preferred future for the church. Where is this leading Stillmeadow?

I heard about a book called the *Bonsai Theory of Church Growth* by Ken

Hemphill. The driving metaphor of the book is that God did not create the bonsai tree. God created trees to grow, but the bonsai tree has been placed in a small pot with an artist intentionally trimming the tree back to keep it small. The application is that most of the things that are limiting our growth are of human origin. Acts 2 reads, "They sat under the apostles' teaching . . . they had fellowship together . . . they took care of one another . . . they broke bread in one another's homes and the Lord added to the church daily those who were being saved" (see vv. 42-47). That's normal church life. We have got to honestly address the human limitations we have put on the church's growth. That's not a pleasant conversation. If the church will do an autopsy so we can see for ourselves what has limited our growth and be willing to take courageous steps to address those human limitations, the future is as bright as the promises of God.

Saturday Night Live

New Life Community Church of the Nazarene
Pismo Beach, California
Ron Salsbury, Pastor

Profile

Following Hurricane Katrina the New Life Community Church of the Nazarene in Pismo Beach, California, contributed the largest offering from a Nazarene congregation ever to a disaster response. On September 11, 2005, the Sunday following Katrina, Pastor Ron Salsbury provided an opportunity for his congregation to give the entire weekend offering to the relief effort; $120,000—twice the weekly average—was given and sent for use by Nazarene Disaster Response in the Gulf Coast region.

On behalf of a grateful denomination I arranged to visit the church to express thanks to the people for this remarkable, generous offering. I brought a video with words of appreciation from General Superintendent J. K. Warrick, who was filmed a few days earlier standing in the rubble surrounding a ruined church in Mississippi.

I arrived in time for the Saturday evening worship. The 970-seat sanctuary was nearly full, as it was for the two Sunday morning services—over 2,200 attended over the weekend. This growing congregation in a small beach community 200 miles north of Los Angeles has found a way to attract and involve otherwise unchurched people in a wide range of neighborhood and distant mission projects.

It was a strong congregation of 900 in an ideal location when Ron and Cathi Salsbury arrived in 1993. From its hillside location, a panoramic glassed lobby overlooks the neighborhood. The sanctuary, recently renovated following an earthquake, fans out in a semicircle. A video screen extends the full length of the stage, bounded by two large crosses—one made from pieces of the stained-glass windows broken during the earthquake; the other made of wood and covered with thousands of nails, each one nailed by those who attended the Holy Week services a year ago.

On the Sunday I attended, the three worship services were led by a casually dressed worship arts team surrounded by carefully arranged plants, artwork, and multiple-candle arrangements in front of draped backdrops. The worship leader, sitting on a stool under a spotlight in a dimly lit sanctuary, accompanied himself on a guitar as he invited us to join him in singing a variety of contemporary choruses and old songs, including an upbeat arrangement of the ancient hymn by Francis of Assisi "All Creatures of Our God and King." The worship experience wasn't loud, rushed, or carefully scripted. It seemed casually contemplative. In one service the worship leader took time to explain that he needed a moment to retune his guitar. This fit just right somehow for a California beach community.

When it was his time, Ron Salsbury came to the podium from his front-row seat, dressed in slacks (blue jeans on Saturday night) and an untucked shirt, to deliver a sermon filled with scriptures displayed on the large screen above and behind him. He taught, humored, testified, and at times invited the audience to talk back. Although following detailed notes, he was clearly at ease with himself and connected to the congregation—a generational mix of generous members engaged in missions.

Conversation with Pastor Ron Salsbury

I know you were once a professional musician. How did it happen that you became a pastor?

I came out of a career in contemporary Christian music. I had gone through a divorce that I did not want. For a number of years I lived in a fellowship house that was a ministry through Los Angeles First Church of the Nazarene. During that time Ron and Randy Benefiel were roommates of mine. I was a volunteer with the single adult ministry and led the worship at the Tuesday night Bible study. God used that experience to bring healing to my life. I got involved in urban ministry in downtown Los Angeles. When Ron Benefiel resigned to finish his Ph.D. at USC, they asked me to come on staff and direct the single adult program. So I went on staff with fear and trembling. I just loved the ministry of working with other people. While I was serving at Los Angeles First and going to school, I met Cathi at the single adult Bible study and we were married in 1983.

I went back to school. I did some undergrad work at Azusa Pacific University, graduated from Fuller Seminary, and was ordained in 1986. When Ron Benefiel returned as senior pastor, I served for two more years but I started having a strong calling to preach. I remember feeling on Sunday morning while Ron was preaching that I'd never be as good as this guy. But I had to preach. I felt like a second-string quarterback that wanted to be traded so he could throw the ball. I talked to the district superintendent and nothing happened for six months. No interest, no calls, nothing. I went through a reverse identity crisis—cut my hair, got a three-piece suit—the opposite of what most guys do. Finally I went to see the district superintendent again and I asked him if there was any church that was interested in me and he said there was—Lancaster in the northern desert and they wanted to talk with me. We went there and fell in love with the people. They had about 90 in attendance, a worship center that seated about 300, and a really good sound system. We went there with two little kids, spent five wonderful years, and saw the church grow to about 350 in attendance—a lot of people coming to Christ. I led worship and preached.

When the call from Pismo Beach came, I really didn't want to go. I was happy in Lancaster. But we came over to interview just to see what God might be saying. We came with fear and trembling—they were running about 900 at the time. That was 13 years ago, January 1993.

What did you find when you came to New Life Community?

They were really focused on outreach. It was a healthy church—worship was a part of their DNA. I led worship and preached for the first five years.

How would you describe your style of worship?

I played guitar. I would call it a celebrative, boomer type of worship.

Was that different for them?

Not really. They were doing contemporary choruses at the time. They had a kind of Pentecostal flavor of worship life—not public tongues, but openness and exuberance and expression. I assumed that kind of openness would translate into trying new things. One of the challenges I faced was that there wasn't always that super openness for doing new things.

Like what?

Like the Wednesday night service—going to small groups—that sort of thing. That was a bit of a surprise to me. I thought that a freedom and openness in worship would translate into a freedom and openness in programmatic change—but that wasn't the case. I fought a couple of battles early on, but then we started to really hit our stride. Now it's been a good run of a number of years just keeping the central mission vision values of our church as our focus.

You added on average about 100 a year for 13 years. How do you sustain that kind of growth?

We've also had a lot of exits. Since the *Purpose-Driven Life* came out, we've added a number of small groups. When that book came out, I did a sermon series on it and we launched a bunch of new groups and went through the book together. We were prepared for 300 people to sign up for groups with leaders, and over 700 signed up. It blew all our systems, so I hired a part-time person just to administer the small groups. Then I thought that what we did after the *Purpose-Driven Life* would be more important than the original launch.

What did you do as the follow-up?

We got some materials from Saddleback—they were already strategizing on some materials for groups to use after *Purpose-Driven Life*. And then we coordinated our recovery groups, support groups—all of the small groups.

How many people in the church are involved in cell groups?

About 40 percent of the church is in small groups.

That would be about a thousand people, right?

Pretty close to it. I guess that's the lower end of the definition of a church *of* small groups instead of just a church *with* small groups. That's what we're trying to be—a church of small groups.

In addition to the groups developed from the Purpose-Driven program, you have other kinds of groups.

All kinds of mission and service groups. We have recovery groups, recreation groups.

Do the groups have a lot of turnover?

You always have to launch new groups. That's one of the keys. There always has to be new entry points for people. You have to make the pathways really clear for serving and membership. So we have a path we call New Life Connections, which meets Friday night and Saturday morning. It has three components: membership, maturity, and ministry. I teach Friday night on membership; it helps people understand what New Life is all about—our mission vision values—and gives them a chance to get to know me and for me to get to know them. Usually there are about 30 to 50 in that class, and we do it once a quarter. If they want to join, they can—but they don't have to. But if they want to join, they have to take that class.

And then on Saturday morning, half of the time is spent on maturity, about how we grow in Christ. The other half is on ministry. We give them some tests and exercises to help them find their place of service.

I presume you are trying to get people who come to worship involved in cell groups.

Yes, cell groups and involved in ministry. We have a little booklet titled "Connected by Service" that helps those who join the church get involved in ministry. John Maxwell once said that second only to the number of conversions the most important statistic in a healthy church is the number of people involved in regular weekly ministry.

What are the primary entry points into New Life? How do people become connected?

I'd say that probably the number one way is the weekend worship. And we have a recovery ministry called Celebrate Recovery on Friday night. People often come to that and then come to the church. We also have big outreach events; we have a huge Fourth of July picnic and of course Christmas and Easter. We invest a lot of money in advertising at Easter and have multiple services. We have a seniors' exercise class called Stretch to Be Fit. That's been a great outreach in the community. Senior adults come to the church through that. We have parents come through children's and youth ministry events. But still the number one way is word of mouth. We're a pretty large church in a fairly small area. Getting people to know about New Life in our area is not a problem. The challenge is to counter the recreational spirit or attitude. We have a lot of people who come occasionally. Getting them to come regularly, not just on Christmas and Easter (I call those people CEOs—Christmas and Easter Only), is the challenge. I try to do that by doing a series of messages and getting them involved in small groups and ministries.

I thought one of the most unusual things was the large attendance on Saturday evening. How do you explain this astounding turnout?

That's something that's been growing. At least 80 percent of the time in the last six months the Saturday night service has been our largest. I think this happens for a couple of reasons. One is that we do live in a beautiful area and a lot of people like to come on Saturday and do something on Sunday. What I've seen, too, is that a lot of families are coming on Saturday night to worship and then making Sunday a family day. I think that has some real advantages.

In his new book *Revolution,* George Barna claims to have documented the phenomenon of committed believers who are not much interested in church as we know it. Is that a trend that you're seeing?

Yes—I think it's almost reverting back to the old parish mentality of the Catholic tradition. There are people that regard themselves as a real active part of New Life even though they only come once a month or once every other month. Many times these people will be involved in volunteer ministries or youth ministry. It's surprising to me that they might connect to the church in other ways but not really be a part of the regular worshiping community. They might be perceived to be somewhat consumerist because they may come only on a weekend when the message is about something they are interested in. But they are not purely consumerist, because they are involved in real active ways of serving.

We're part of a ministry called People's Kitchen that serves hot meals 365 days a year. It was actually birthed out of New Life, but there are many churches that are a part of it now. I know a lot of people who are active in serving in People's Kitchen and we see them very sporadically. It's something that concerns me. In the old paradigm a center circle would be the worship experience and then the smaller circles that connect to the center circle would be the ministry opportunities that you can explore spanning from the weekend worship time—that would be small groups, Sunday School, service, fellowship, all these different things. But for the emerging church the central point is community expressed in serving together. And then one of the connecting circles would be some kind of weekly gathering. So it's kind of flip-flopped. The central thing for the emerging church is to come together to serve and then find other avenues for the worship experience.

How did you get people to contribute $120,000 on one Sunday for Katrina relief?

That was about twice as much as we normally receive on a really good Sunday. I've told my people many times that God didn't call me to fund-raising but fun-raising. When you get a spirit of generosity for investing in stuff that's really cool, it's fun. I think the old method of fund-raising in the church was, "If you give, we can do this." The new motivation is, "Because you gave, we were able do this." So we've developed a yearly expectation that we're going to report to them all the different ministries we've supported. We used to do it just on a weekend with a PowerPoint presentation, but now we're trying to do it more often throughout the year.

We heard that Saddleback had the goal of sending out 10 percent of their weekend attendance into mission work every year. That challenged us, so our leadership adopted the same goal for our church. We have about 2,000 on a weekend, so I said this year I'd like to send out about 200 into mission work somewhere foreign or domestic. We're passing 175 now. We're going to hit our goal I think.

Where do they go on these mission trips?

I have a young couple reporting this weekend that went to Bosnia. Some of the youth trips have been to Mexico. We have a high school group that went to inner-city Chicago. We have lots of groups that go down to Central City in Los Angeles. We've been able to help every student that's asked for support in the last few years. Every student and adult that wants to go, we try to help in some way. We have groups going to work in the Gulf Coast and another group taking the *JESUS* film to India.

As I've said, we do lots of reporting on what we're doing with the church's money. That's a key thing. And that's why Dr. Warrick's thank-you has probably done as much for our church's missionary giving as anything else ever has, because to say thank you is so motivating—because you gave we were able to do this. To show what we did with the money is so much more motivating than the old style of "If you give, we can do this."

How has your style of ministry changed as the church has grown?

When I went to New Life, all of my mentors said don't work on your weaknesses, spend most of your time doing what you do well and get others to help with the other areas. So I've tried from day one to develop a team approach. I'd say that more and more I really focus on what I do well.

Which is?

The weekend—teaching and preaching. And mentoring and developing young men. I try to spend my time strategically so that I'm not just available to everybody who wants to see me. I'm in the office Tuesday, Wednesday, and Thursday afternoons, and most of Tuesday afternoon is spent working with the worship arts department. We pray, evaluate, and plan. So more and more of my time is spent discipling guys. What energizes me is discipling pre-Christian or new Christian guys. That's the evangelist in me. I'm a horrible counselor, but I do pretty well at discipling men. I'm thankful that we have a care department that does most of our counseling.

Is there anything else?

Just that I'm so thankful for a church that would ordain me after coming from a place of brokenness. When I went through the divorce—I can still remember the day; I get kind of choked up when I tell it—but Ron Benefiel pulled up to my house in an ugly little green Fiat and took me to lunch and invited me to come to a Bible study. At that point in my life I thought my ministry usefulness was over. He reached out to me, discipled me, and got me involved in ministry, and when it came time to be ordained, I submitted to my local, district, and general church leadership. I had to explain what happened and so forth. But they took a risk on me. And I'm thankful for that. For the rest of my life I'll be able to minister to broken people and tell them that there's a church that gives people another chance. It's all about grace. We're just offering to others what we've received ourselves.

Sunday Night Jail

Trevecca Community Church of the Nazarene
Nashville
Dwight Gunter, Pastor

Profile

The Trevecca Community Church of the Nazarene (TCCN) is located off seedy Murfreesboro Road in Nashville inside the expansive new entrance to Trevecca Nazarene University. The church serves as a buffer of sorts between the university community and a troubled urban neighborhood.

I arrived one Sunday morning at the same time as a busload of men from a halfway house. Some were lingering outside the main entrance of the church for one last drag on their cigarettes before entering. They were easy to spot among the regulars dressed in church clothes. It was their first Sunday too.

I asked the man who was giving directions about where to find the coffee, the bathrooms, and meeting room if I could join the group. I decided that with his attire—bare tattooed arms under a biker's leather vest—I should at least take off my tie so as not to appear too churchy.

This was the first Sunday for a new recovery ministry to men from a nearby halfway house—all of them recently imprisoned convicts about to be released. A similar group of women had been attending for some time. Several of the more than 100 men and women attending the recovery groups were baptized, and some joined the church that morning.

Under the leadership of Dwight Gunter the church is finding creative ways of building bridges between worlds, bringing people together who would otherwise never encounter one another. TCCN is now home to university professors, staff, and students; residents of Trevecca Towers—a retirement community a block away; a cross section of Nashville citizens; and an increasing number of marginalized people for whom Murfreesboro Road is home.

Applying strategies he studied and documented in his doctor of ministry dissertation on change and transition in local congregations, Gunter has been able to lead the established church members through significant changes as they understand what it means to be about God's mission in the world.

Near the end of his high school days Gunter was close to his dream of an appointment to the Air Force Academy. A call to preach changed the direction of his life. After completing his college and seminary studies in 1982, he served in several pastoral assignments until coming to TCCN in 2002.

Conversation with Pastor Dwight Gunter

George Barna has included you in his inner circle and sees Trevecca Community as one of a few so-called revolutionary churches—churches where people who are dropping out of the church are inclined to go. What makes your church unique?

It is an issue of the church truly being the church. George Barna has discovered this, Reggie McNeal has discovered it, and it's in *The Organic Church* by Neil Cole. They all talk about it. People are leaving the church for a new reason. They are leaving it to preserve their faith. And it's not a radical, individualistic issue of the church not giving them what they wanted. George Barna discovered that there are seven facets of a revolutionary. So the revolutionaries come to this church, and they say, "Well, this church is doing what it's supposed to be doing, and therefore, I'm in line with this church."

What had to change at Trevecca Community to align with those revolutionary mission objectives?

This may not be the answer you're looking for, Tom—but the people at TCCN were hungry for this. I came in and said we need to reorganize. They wanted to cut the size of the board. I know churches get in trouble and pastors get criticized for trying to reduce the size of the church board. But they said, you did your dissertation on it—bring us a recommendation.

What was your dissertation about?

It was "Leading a Church Through Organizational Transition Within a Changing Vision." The whole idea was about creating a mission-centered church that in and of itself would achieve the desired end, that being the mission of God in the world.

You were able to write a thesis that had some practical application in your ministry.

It really did work for us.

A lot of churches lose people in a transition. What about here?

We didn't lose anyone. We gained. We reorganized around the purposes of the church. We showed that administration is not at the top of the organizational grid; it is at the bottom to resource people to accomplish their purposes. We cut the size of the board from about 22 down to 12, and that's including the department heads. And we increased participation in the life of the church by establishing ministry action teams. So instead of having 22 people that were involved in the leadership of the church, we ended up with about 70 people in leadership. So we increased participation in the leadership significantly, and then beyond that I began to preach and teach the biblical mission and purpose of the church. And I do that regularly. I do it every year. In fact, I constantly talk about our purpose. This is what the people of God are to be. We talk about belonging. We talk about people who are hurting. If we've had anyone who said, "Well, if you bring those people in here, I'm leaving," I never heard it.

The Sunday I visited I sat in on a remarkable Sunday School class—a group of people from a halfway house. How did they come to attend Sunday School at Trevecca Community?

I got a phone call one night saying, "Pastor, the police have the paddy wagon in our parking lot, and they're loading it up with prostitutes they're arresting on the streets. And we have youth and children coming in and out of here for activities." So I came down and said to the police, "I appreciate what you're doing, but we don't want the church associated with a place where people are arrested. We want the church associated with redemption; we don't want someone to remember the church as the place they were arrested." At about the same time, I attended a meeting of a business association here in our area, and they brought up the problem of prostitution. It's right on the streets in front of our church, and one of the businessmen said, "I don't care where they go; I just want them out from in front of my business." God convicted my heart over that issue. I thought—we shouldn't be driving them somewhere else. We have to redeem them. We have to help them, and I don't know how to help them. In the next Sunday's sermon God brought that scene to my mind, and I shared that story with our congregation. I said to them, "I don't know what to do. I have no clue. I'm not an inner-city pastor. I don't know how to do this ministry, but God has to send us someone who does and has to somehow raise a ministry, because I know it's breaking the heart of God, and we can't say, 'Just go work another street. Leave us alone.'"

I met some of your leaders who are now working with people

from the street, halfway houses, and jails. How did they find their ministry here?

God led a woman who had come through a recovery ministry for prostitutes to our church. The Sunday she visited I was preaching on the prostitute washing the feet of Jesus with her tears and drying them with her hair and anointing His feet with perfume in the home of Simon the Pharisee (see Luke 7:36-50). And she said, "When you read that text, I knew I had found my church." She eventually joined and started bringing other people. Our congregation was so moved by that, that they said, "What can we do?" And she said to us, "Let's start a jail ministry. Let's go to the prisons one night a week." At the same time God sent us a lady—an ordained elder—who joined our staff. Pastor Tina Mitchell was obedient to a burden God placed on her—a call to minister to the disenfranchised of our streets. Those two visions merged, and it became crystal clear that all this was first God's vision. So we started services for women in jail with about 30 attending; now there are over 100 that attend the Sunday night service in the jail. And out of that we are training workers for Celebrate Recovery. Recently we began services in the men's jail. God is blessing, and lives are being transformed. I think there are about 45 men attending that service (which is about two months old).

It's one thing to get your people to go the jails; it must be another challenge to invite in people from halfway houses.

We asked a woman—she is in charge of the justice system dealing with community networks—to teach a relapse prevention group for women on Sunday nights. Her husband is now teaching it for men in our church on Sunday nights. We are still going into the jails. But we're up to about 100 men and women who attend the support groups for relapse prevention, spiritual support, and services that include helping them find a place to live, helping them get set up in their apartments when they get out of halfway houses, helping them find jobs, getting them clothes, and furnishing their apartments.

Our people are doing all of that, and that doesn't even count what we're doing in our neighborhood, such as partnering with the inner-city elementary school around the corner in tutoring math and reading, and we have senior adults who live at the Towers and students from Trevecca who go down to that area to help. We run a King's Kids (mentoring) program where we hook up college students with children from the area, and we run that every Tuesday night during the school year. And that's about to expand to an all-summer program. Pastor Tina has a great vision for the expansion of that ministry. We'll have 75 to 100 kids attending that are mentored by college students.

It must be tough leading a church with the university and retirement center on one side and Murfreesboro Road on the other. What's that like?

Nashville has cleaned up a lot of their inner-city projects. They've moved the problem people out here. They made them leave, and so they left and went right here to Murfreesboro Road. Gang violence has become an issue. We're partnering with other agencies to try to address this as well. It is a challenge, but God has called His people to go into His world. The heart of the university and the retirement center is pulled toward this ministry as well. So the challenge is more logistical and programmatic than one of convincing people of God's vision.

You drive through that every day when you go to church.

Yeah, it's every day. There's gang violence here because a lot of old gangs have moved into this area. Our people drive in from one of the richest counties in our nation. They come from affluent areas of Nashville, all because they believe in the mission of the church. We're doing everything we can to help. I believe this is a theological issue. I believe that sanctification is so much more than an individual matter. When Paul said, "May God himself, the God of peace, sanctify you through and through" [1 Thess. 5:23], he wasn't just talking to individuals; he was talking to the church. I believe that the church has to be sanctified, be set apart, become Christlike, in order to go *into* a community. That community is then sanctified, so to speak, by the very presence of God through the church. And if sanctification is dealing with transformation—and that's what we've taught and preached all of our existence, that we are transformed by the renewing of our minds—then we as a church can help, can be used by God to sanctify a community, in essence, to transform that community into something more like God.

How do you preach to such a diverse congregation—the college community, commuters from the suburbs, and people from halfway houses?

I try to establish rapport with the congregation, a relationship to draw them into the story. I don't have any one approach. It's down-to-earth. It is authentic. I speak from my heart. I try to be open with people and talk about my own struggles—the issues that I face.

In the sermon I heard you were open enough to talk about disagreements between you and your wife.

That's the authenticity part. That kind of realism is where life is. Board members, people off the streets, people trying to deal with addictions—they argue with their family, and so if you want to deal with these people where they are, you identify with them. I don't make stuff up, but I do identify with them. I just try to be open, authentic, and real, and say to them, it's OK to be open and honest and real, and that's the only way we're truly going to grow.

How do you plan a worship experience to attract people from such different backgrounds?

We sing hymns and choruses, we have dramas, we do video, we do all the PowerPoint stuff. We appeal to different learning styles. We try to use culturally relevant norms and mediums to communicate the message. We do high church things. We do informal kinds of things. We are thematic and try to create a biblical narrative centered on that theme. We believe God is the object of our worship. He is the audience. We are to worship Him and we do that in ways that try to fit people, which is a real challenge. In our community you have a large variety just with students; it's even larger when you add in a retirement community, a street community, and a business community, you know, middle-aged business community. So it is an incredible challenge. I've never had a congregation as diverse as this, with different nationalities, different races, and then a huge diversity along socioeconomic lines.

A lot of people have been added to the fellowship in the four years you've been here.

We have grown. We were running just under 400 when I arrived here, and now during the school year we are running over 800.

That's a lot of new people to absorb.

It is—and that has been our biggest challenge. We did the Natural Church Development survey where we looked at the weakest link in our church as a measure of church health. Some people say church health is an outdated metaphor, but it still works for us. We found that in all categories we were above the healthy mark. However, we were weakest in relationships, and so we have worked hard at trying to build relationships among people. We have organized ministries and programs that help get people together. One of the greatest things about this church is that it's immediately accepting and you feel you belong when you walk in. There's always the challenge of building relationships among people, and relationships are just like anything else—if you don't tend them, they will deteriorate.

Too Big for Potlucks

Oro Valley Church of the Nazarene
Oro Valley, Arizona
Craig Coulter, Pastor

Profile

A few miles north of Tucson in an upper-middle-class neighborhood, the Oro Valley, Arizona, Church of the Nazarene has more than doubled in attendance to over 700 since Craig Coulter came to pastor in 2001. That year the 25-year-old congregation was waiting to grow. The church was in a good location, had strong children's and youth programs, and was holding three Sunday morning worship services in a small sanctuary. In 2003 the congregation constructed a new 650-seat sanctuary that they entered through a courtyard surrounded by their other buildings.

Following graduation from MidAmerica Nazarene University in 1985 and Nazarene Theological Seminary in 1989, Craig and Robin served churches in East Texas and Kansas before accepting the invitation to Oro Valley.

On the Saturday before my Sunday visit, the church organized a workday to refurbish a shelter for homeless people in Tucson. It was the conclusion of their "40 Days of Community," a program to organize church members and visitors in small groups for community outreach and spiritual direction. In both services (the church now meets for two services instead of three) while watching a video of children, youth, and families giving their Saturday to this compassion program, the people celebrated what God had accomplished through them.

Their rapid growth is a result of maximizing the use of their good location and facilities in a growing suburban neighborhood. Pastor Coulter has successfully led the church members to understand the interests and needs of the people they are trying to reach. In some ways it's a traditional Nazarene congregation that has found a way to use its heritage as a bridge to unchurched people from a variety of religious traditions.

Pastor Coulter is aware that this growing congregation is very much a work in progress. He readily admits that they are searching for new effective ways of reaching and retaining new people. They are struggling to find a small-group program that works for them. Their vision combined with their core values is leading them to an unknown but exciting future.

Conversation with Pastor Craig Coulter

What were your first impressions when you came to the Oro Valley church?

I found that it had a vision. They knew what God wanted them to do and where they were headed. But they had gone through a tough transition. We had three services on Sunday morning, with a small sanctuary that seated 150 people. They had some money set aside to build a new building, but they didn't quite have the direction about what size the building should be. The vision was in place, but they needed help to get there. There were about 350 in attendance when I came. Now there are about 700—the church had doubled in 5 years.

How do you account for the growth from 350 in 2001 to over 700 today?

We've had a well-rounded ministry. We had a good children's ministry, a good youth ministry, and a strong worship ministry. The pieces were in line for growth to take place. It was also the people's openness to change.

We realized when we were building the sanctuary that people really liked the small sanctuary—they felt comfortable with it. We motivated people by reminding them that we weren't building the sanctuary for us—we kept saying—we're building it for people who have not yet come to our church. When we went into the new sanctuary seating 650 people, we decided we needed to keep two services. That was a huge paradigm shift for people who thought that one day we're going to enter the Promised Land—going from three services to one service in the morning. But it was amazing how people stepped up and said, "We're not doing this for us; we're doing it for others."

What other changes contributed to the growth?

We have limited Sunday School areas, so when we went from three to two morning services, it meant a lot of shifting around—but people were willing to change. People's thinking changed from being a small church to a growing church. That caused us to expand our horizon—we had to change the way we think. Process and improvement is something we always talk about. The biggest change we're going through right now, the thing we're struggling with, is how to do small groups.

Why is that a struggle?

Because we feel we don't want to use people to the point that they're exhausted and don't have time to reach out to others. Scheduling small groups means that we limit to some extent our Sunday night services. People love our Sunday nights. We would pack out our old sanctuary almost every Sunday night. It was a vibrant time for the church. But when we began small groups, we decided to have just two Sunday night services a month. We know that small groups is one of the key ways that we'll be growing our church through fellowship and assimilation. We know we have to get there.

Will the groups organized in your "40 Days of Community" continue?

We told those in the groups that if they want to continue, we'll provide direction and curriculum. I get really controlling about this. I want to control what our small groups are studying. We told them we'll give them curriculum, we'll support them, but they'll have to have certain qualifications. We didn't want to have just anybody starting a small group.

I heard something interesting from the teacher of the adult Sunday School class I attended. He talked about dividing his rather large class into small groups. That's interesting.

There is no way to get away from our being a traditional Nazarene church with a very successful Sunday School—but all we have room for are large classes rather than small groups.

How do you plan your worship experiences?

We're in a transition. Right now I'm the one that provides the direction for each service. Our worship pastor keeps a schedule of different things, and we get together twice a month. I went to a conference at Ed Young's church that was so challenging—his whole theme is, "It's all about Sunday morning." Being creative, doing things that create that experience—it's like you said—people in break-out churches have the feeling that if they don't go to worship, they're going to miss something. For that to happen it takes a tremendous amount of planning and looking ahead. We get so busy doing the everyday stuff that we forget how to be creative. I don't do real well at this, but as best I can, I try to look ahead and say, "Here's a testimony that would fit with that sermon." Likewise, when we knew we were going to have this Saturday workday, I said, "We want to have a video put to music." We're just on the edge of being creative—we're not really there.

I noticed that you served Communion on the side of the sanctuary for a few people.

When we moved into the new sanctuary, it provided us an opportunity to make some changes in the way we do worship. We target people who used to have a religious background but somehow have drifted away from that and now they're coming back because they're having families or getting married or going through some other transition. They're coming back to try church out one more time to see if it really would make a difference. We have people coming to our church with all kinds of different religious backgrounds. Some of them are looking for Communion every Sunday. If it's important to them, why wouldn't we provide it? We just decided that every Sunday there would be Communion. There were some reservations, but no one has come to me and said I don't like that at all. After the sermon we have a time of response when people can take Communion—about 50 people do each Sunday—or pray at the altar. We want people to worship in a way that they feel comfortable.

Your sermon was in the middle of the service rather than at the end. Is it that way every Sunday?

When we were in our small sanctuary with three services, we had to get done in one hour. We had a traditional Nazarene order of worship—music, prayer time, offering, offertory special, and the sermon. When I got done, I'd tell people to run out of there because we had other people coming in. When we made the transition to the new sanctuary, I realized it was an opportunity to change the schedule. Here's what we do. We have about 15 to 20 minutes of worship singing, followed by the announcements, and then I get up real early in the service. We wanted the spoken Word at the center of the service—early in the service rather than during the last half. We come back to worship after I am done speaking. It was a bit of an awkward transition because we weren't used to having something after my sermon. But we feel that that has helped our worship experience.

How do you describe your preaching?

I don't think I'm incredibly deep with my preaching. I try to speak to a lot of people. I try my best not to speak down to them or to be judgmental. I try to be encouraging and yet I don't like to pull punches—I don't like to sugarcoat things. I want them to know what God's Word says. If it means they need to make some changes, great, but I try to say that in an encouraging way.

I noticed that you're very extemporaneous even with your sermon notes.

Here's part of my struggle with that. I feel I have so much stuff I want to get out there that I start shooting from the hip and find that my time goes really fast. I try to make sure I get to the main points. I go to the platform with a full manuscript before me. I have a large pulpit—I sometimes walk to the side and speak directly to the congregation, but most of the time I'm behind the pulpit. I'm a bit more traditional in my delivery.

What is the profile of the target group in Oro Valley you're trying to reach?

Oro Valley is an upper-middle-class bedroom community for Tucson, with lots of professionals—lots of people who work at Raytheon (many engineers go to our church here)—extremely busy people with families. If they're really busy, we want to make sure that the time they give us will make an impact in their lives. We talk about family relationships a lot. We have a great youth and children's program. And we have another totally different group in the three large retirement communities in the Oro Valley area. When we sing a hymn—we always make it a point to sing one hymn in each service—there are a lot of people that perk up and start singing really loud. Our target groups are young families and middle-aged families looking for something for their kids—for something real in their lives that reminds them of that religious experience when they were growing up and ministers to where they're at right now.

What's the future for the church?

It's pretty bright at our church—we believe with all our hearts that the best is yet to come. Soon we'll fill up the two Sunday morning services and start a Saturday night service. I feel that with the blurring of Sunday as a nonworking day there are all kinds of people who have to work on Sundays now. They're looking for something they can do on Saturday. We know that we need to meet that need. Another thing, when we get our new children's and youth wing built, we want to take our old sanctuary and retrofit it back as it was and have more of a traditional service with a high-definition screen through which to project the sermon. Out just a bit further we'll implement the multisite concept. We don't want to become a huge box church somewhere five miles north of here. This is going to be our main site; additional sites will be equipped with pastoral staff, but the preaching on Sunday will be connected so that we're all going in the same direction.

What will have to change for you to get there?

The hardest thing to change is the paradigm that says, "This is the way church is done." There's that constant struggle between "This is the way we've always done it" and "This is what we see God could do if we changed."

We recently had a five-hour Saturday board Vision Day meeting in which we talked about major changes needed in our church. One was restructuring how we do our board meetings and the structure of church board and staff. We're working through the whole paradigm shift from the church board making all the decisions to a church board that becomes an overseer of the vision. The board would make sure we're on track with our core values and with tying the budget to where we need to go—but then it would allow the staff to manage the church. Making this change is a huge struggle.

We need to make some decisions now about our future building plans. We've outgrown the idea that the whole church can fellowship together at one time in one place. We're at a size where having a big fellowship in which everybody comes for a big potluck is impossible.

Signs of Pentecost and Heaven

Crossroads Tabernacle Church of the Nazarene
Fort Worth
Corey Jones, Pastor
and
The Risen Lamb International Church of the
Nazarene
Kansas City, Kansas
Dorzell King, Pastor

Profile

What are the prospects for inclusive churches in a multicultural society? I fear that unless local churches and denominational centers look more like our increasingly diverse society, they risk becoming marginalized, isolated, culturally specific religious communities in a multicultural world.

In October 2006, the United States population reached 300 million, growing at 1 percent, or 3 million, annually—this is equal to a city the size of Chicago every year. Immigration and high birth rates among immigrant and minority groups is fueling the growth. The United States population will reach 400 million by mid-century. Canada's population of 33 million is growing at a similar rate with even more diversity. There is no one-majority group in the total population of the 100 largest cities in the United States as the country becomes more urban and culturally diverse.

As America struggles to find its new multicultural identity with no dominant culture, could it be that the health and growth of churches depends on how much they look like our neighborhoods, shopping malls, airports, and schools?

There are new signs of hope. Leaders of various people groups are increasingly respected and followed by the general population. In the church world many congregations are successfully expanding their membership and mission beyond their own cultural or language group.

Since more than half of the 1,000-plus new Nazarene churches in the past decade have been started among immigrant and other culturally specific groups, there are more leaders from these groups available for denominational leadership positions. They have been elected to district advisory boards and have been appointed and elected to other leadership positions.

However, the increasing number of culturally specific churches adds to worship segregation. These churches are safe places where people gather in familiar enclaves, removed from work, school, and other places where they are forced to adapt to the dominant culture. Even non-Hispanic white churches remain the one place where people in the dominant culture are not threatened by their loss of identity.

It's not clear which are most viable—culturally specific or culturally blended congregations. Trends outside the church have much to say about what works best inside the church. All kinds of churches are needed to respond to the ways people choose to come to faith and discipleship and decide which churches to attend.

The criteria by which all churches can be evaluated as authentic communities of Christian faith is the degree to which they use culture as a barrier or a bridge to the gospel. An authentic Christian community will never use its culture, either intentionally or unintentionally, to exclude others. The work of a missionary church is always to cross language, cultural, and belief barriers to announce the Good News and build a church that welcomes all God's children.

There are times when churches need to challenge rather than mirror society. As people come to faith and discipleship, they are introduced to a new community and, however imperfect, a sign of God's kingdom present and coming.

The memory and experience of Pentecost when the Spirit of God infused a crowd made up of people from many countries provides the spiritual foundation of this new community. Pentecost is a sign of God's inclusive church—already and not yet. To pray for God's will to be done on earth as it is in heaven is to begin now to incarnate the hope of heaven where all the tribes of earth are gathered around the risen Lord.

In the occasional denominational event with people from many different congregations, languages, and cultures we are often reminded that such inclusive gatherings are a foretaste of heaven. There are a few congregations where the Pentecostal promise and heavenly vision are being lived out even now.

Recently I saw these signs of Pentecost and heaven in two new, growing multicultural congregations—one in Fort Worth and the other in Kansas City, Kansas. Each has grown to about the same size, with a worship attendance around 400 comprised of several people groups.

After visiting these churches I talked with founding pastors Corey Jones (white) from Crossroads Tabernacle Church of the Nazarene in Fort Worth and Dorzell King (African-American) at the Risen Lamb International Church of the Nazarene in Kansas City about their inclusive, multicultural congregations.

Conversation with Pastor Corey Jones

How did your vision for a multicultural church develop for you?

I really believe the vision was planted in me as a child in my father's churches. He had a large bus ministry in his church, and as a young child I would ride the bus with him. Children and families from different cultural backgrounds were welcome and loved by my father.

That was the seed, but it wasn't until I was in Texas doing graduate work that I had a sudden and dramatic experience that really sparked the vision in me. My wife, Beth Ann, and I had just moved to Texas and we were planting a church in a very affluent and growing suburb of Fort Worth. But one day while I was in my office studying, I heard Beth Ann in the living room crying. She was watching this story on the *700 Club* about a man by the name of Calvin Hunt, from Brooklyn, who had been delivered from crack cocaine. The documentary recounted this man's life of addiction to crack and also how the church where his family went began to fervently pray for him. Amazingly, through the power of a praying church Calvin was delivered.

After watching that program, Beth and I were in tears and we felt God's presence in the room in a very real and distinct way. We began to feel God really speaking to us about being part of a church that reached out to people just like Calvin Hunt. That day God changed our plans. But it wasn't really a vision for a multicultural church that God gave us that day but simply a heart of compassion for hurting and broken people. That's how it began.

How old is the Crossroads congregation?

We celebrated our 10th anniversary in March 2006. The church started in 1994 as a suburban small group made up entirely of young affluent white folks. But in 1995 after witnessing that story about Calvin Hunt's deliverance from crack, we asked our small group to change directions with us. It wasn't long before we found a building in East Fort Worth that was perfect for what God had for us.

When did you come to this building?

In March 1996, we began with about 25 people. Most of the families

from the original small group came with us. But the church building was in total disrepair and only about three families were left in
the congregation that at the time was called the Meadowbrook
Church of the Nazarene.

What was the neighborhood like back then?

You often hear about the so-called train tracks that seemingly divide
the affluent suburbs from the inner city. Well, we thought we were
right on the tracks. There were very nice homes across the street from
the church, but then behind us and really all around the church were
low-income apartments. Also, the neighborhood was very diverse culturally with a tremendous number of African-Americans.

It was perfect for the vision God had given us. We knew that
God must have had this place in mind when He changed our plans,
but honestly we were really overwhelmed by all the tremendously
diverse needs in our neighborhood.

**After 10 years the congregation is a fascinating mix of middle
to upper-middle-class whites who are committed to ministry to
that neighborhood with all of its problems. How did that happen?**

After we relocated and changed directions, we lost many of those
first families that originally went with us. But the white families
that stayed with us are here because they felt called and believed in
the vision. God spoke to Beth and me early on to reach out and love
those who couldn't give a thing to our church, and with that we believed God's promise to bring people of means because they'll see
what He is able to do. When white, upwardly mobile families come,
they at first may be uncomfortable with the mix but they're amazed
at the miracles and at what God is doing in the people's lives.
They're seeing God doing something in people's lives that they've
never seen anyone else do. No social agency; no program. Here are

people that society doesn't seem to have any solutions for and yet the Lord himself does.

Are the people in your congregation unique, or do you think that there are more upwardly mobile white families in America who want to join culturally and economically mixed congregations?

I think so. I remember hearing Jim Cymbala say that the Lord had put it on his heart that if he would reach the needy and hurting people in Brooklyn, the Lord would send lawyers, doctors—people of means—just to come and see the amazing miracles God can do.

I noticed that you have prosperous Black people as well.

Sure. The middle-class neighborhoods are very diverse. We just built a new home not far from the church, and I am the minority on my street. Over the years we have seen a growing number of middle-class Black people come.

Is your target audience the marginalized?

In the first 10 years we almost exclusively targeted the marginalized.

What about now?

I would say that we continue to be who we were. We don't have any systematic plan to reach so-called upwardly mobile people. We just keep reaching those who walk through the door. One significant outreach was to the homeless last month. Jesus was led to the needy and the hurting—yet people like the rich young ruler would come to Him because of the things they saw Him do. And I really believe that's the situation—people come because they're seeing something God's doing that's unexplainable.

Most of what we hear would indicate that intercultural, eco-

nomically diverse congregations experience some level of tension. Has that been your experience at Crossroads Tabernacle?

It's amazing—the truth is there seems to be very little, if any, disunity or dissention among us. And I completely attribute this lack of disunity to prayer. Prayer brings unity as nothing else can.

Do you address cultural or economic problems directly?

In 10 years I've only had to deal with one problem having cultural implications.

Do you preach about it?

No. I don't ever preach about inclusiveness or being multicultural.

What do you say to pastors with churches surrounded by multicultural neighborhoods?

Well—the kids are the easiest to reach. If you want to reach people, just go out and reach the children. For the first few years the middle-class white families in the area would have nothing to do with us. I saw the BMWs pull into the lot and drive off. Also, if you try to reach a culture other than your own, you're probably not going to reach the adults at first because they're going to observe and watch you for a number of years. Certainly, the ones who are most reachable are children and youth.

In 1996 our church was empty and, as I said, nobody new was coming, so we began to reach out to the low-income apartments through a ministry we call the Peanut Butter and Jelly Kids Club. We have a school bus (with PB&J painted in bold colors on both sides) that picks up hundreds of kids from the apartments and brings them to church every week. Through the constant apartment and street outreaches we began to grow and reach many different cultural groups. Today, our youth ministry is made up of mostly at-risk African-American teenagers.

Who are you trying to reach?

I don't like to answer this question because I feel we are trying to reach everyone. But I would say that we have a real drawing toward people who are different from myself, both economically and culturally. I recently baptized a Black woman from a very bad neighborhood. She represents a large group of people who have simply stopped going to church—and are out there. They will tell you they go to their mother's church or their family's church, but for all intents and purposes they've quit going. They probably are in their 30s, and they have three or four reasons why they have given up on church. Whatever those reasons are, this place seems to overcome those objections. We're reaching a group of people who have faith and have a background in faith but just don't go to church.

Several of your people mentioned the importance of the Tuesday night prayer meeting. What goes on there?

It is truly a prayer meeting. For two hours each Tuesday our congregation comes together to cry out to God. We'll enter with praise—there's no opening; people just come in and stand and begin praising Him. Then we'll go into some worship time—we call it "entering in"—in which different people lead out in prayer; for the next hour we'll lift up needs that are concerning us. We may break into small prayer groups—or there may be some specific people who need prayer—and then I'll share a word of instruction, encouragement, or correction, whatever the Lord leads me to do.

All of our body life is on Tuesday—baptisms, Communion every month. Our Tuesday prayer is a culture for us—not a program. And it is what caused our church to turn the corner and not die. Tuesday night is the most important service of our week, and I honestly believe it really determines the level of victory we have on Sunday.

How do you keep encouraged?

I believe that God has to do something life altering—like a burning bush—for the pastor to keep going. Oliver Phillips* told me that I'm trying to plant the hardest possible kind of church. He said that most white people won't want this and most Black people won't want this either. Then Larry Lott† told me that Black people are going to watch you for five or six years before they ever start coming.

They were both right! In fact, quite a few years back I became extremely discouraged. On the verge of quitting I went out to Brooklyn and stayed with Calvin Hunt,‡ the guy who was delivered from crack. After watching his story on the *700 Club,* Calvin and I met and became good friends. I went and stayed with him and went to his church in Queens, a daughter church of the Brooklyn Tabernacle. On a Tuesday night prayer meeting God showed up and gave me the inspiration and empowerment to keep going. God has really used Calvin and his wife, Miriam, in our lives over the years. They are considered the spiritual mom and dad of our church. And along the way they helped me understand how to do this—because I had no model for it.

Conversation with Pastor Dorzell King

When did you begin the Risen Lamb church?

We started in March 2003 with a launch service. It was sort of a parachute situation because we didn't have a lot of time for core group building. I had about two months of prayer meetings once a week with a group of five to eight people—and then I took two months off to get married.

---

*Director of Mission Strategy for USA/Canada Mission/Evangelism Department, Church of the Nazarene.

†Pastor, Blue Hills Church of the Nazarene, Kansas City.

‡On staff at the Brooklyn Tabernacle.

How did you happen to be in this building?

The members of the Metropolitan, the former congregation, felt they had come to the place where it was time to dissolve as a church but they wanted to pass the property on to another ministry—so the pastor of the church contacted me. The building where we started became the site of another new church; we gave the keys to a Spanish-speaking congregation and they're thriving—they were blessed as well.

When we opened at this new location, we added the word *International* to emphasize our vision—our heart to strive for a multidemographic ministry. We thought that to add that word brought it home.

How many people attend now?

About 400 people in our two worship services.

That includes about an equal number of Black and white people.

Right—those are our two main groups. But as we continue, we really want to pull in more Hispanics—particularly the intermarried families.

What in your calling inspired you to be intentionally multicultural?

I'm not sure that was always in my head, but I think at some point—when I was in high school—I noticed the people that would come out to hear me preach and I observed the impact of seeing different kinds of people worshipping together. I became aware of the prejudice in Black churches as well as white churches, but I grew up in a multicultural church with a white pastor, so I didn't realize the impact it was making on me to be in a church with different kinds of people. It wasn't until about a year ago that I began to realize that my vision of the church was shaped by my experience as a child.

When you were a child, did this seem different to you?

It was not. For me it was normal to go to church with lots of different people—to be in a children's program with white and Hispanic children—and after leaving that and being in an all-white or all-Black context, I began to revisit that vision. I was brought up in a blended church. I realized the Lord was able to bring different types of people together with the ministry He had given me, and I knew then that was the direction we needed to go.

Your church is in a semirural area where most people have to commute. To what degree are the people here because it is intercultural?

For most of them a part of the experience here is worshipping in this context. We have a number of bicultural couples, bicultural children. It seems to me that there is a need for this; they have a hard time finding a church where no one feels alienated.

Other than the bicultural couples, do Black and white people socialize?

They do. We do things to encourage this. We have fellowship dinners for the whole church after services. We have women's and men's ministries to provide opportunities to connect other than Sunday morning. You don't see Black families who have a hard time hanging out with white families or vice versa—there isn't that challenge here. Once you come and have an encounter with the Holy Spirit, something becomes more important than that. It's almost as though you look up and see, Oh, there are a lot of white people here, or there are a lot of Black people here. You notice that later. And then when you do notice it, you say, Oh, I feel so good and comfortable here.

What is unique about Risen Lamb?

I think there is a very special presence of God here. It's expressed in the worship and preaching.

How do you preach?

Maybe conversational. It's important that every sermon conclude with an application to the story of our lives. I intentionally talk about the stories of our lives that aren't so pretty—including my story and the lives of others—because I believe that people think that those are stories that churches are not willing to talk about.

For example?

We can talk about divorce and not make you feel penalized because you went through divorce. One Mother's Day when we honored all the mothers, I asked if we had any teenagers who are mothers. We had one particular mother who stood up and we gave her a flower and blessed her, and I told her, "I'm a child of a 16-year-old mother. Being a teenage mother is a reality. And we just want you to know we're glad you're here." We don't glamorize these realities. But we do go after them and let people know that God really does have something to say about these issues.

How do you describe your worship experience?

The music is very critical. We have about 15 or 20 minutes of worship that flows. We really work to have a seamless experience. I don't like "mental whiplash" or mental hiccups—stop-and-start stuff; I like worship to start and just flow so the worship experience is energetic but not something that will alienate a visitor or an observer. Our transition time from praise and worship to taking the offering and preparing for preaching is always a time of spontaneity and prayer. I think it is important that although every worship service is planned, we're also planning on the unexpected—whether that means testimonies or more singing.

What is your biggest challenge?

First it's tracking. We have so many visitors that we are consistently asking how we are keeping track of people. The other is pulling people into services. Since people live so far away, when we try to bring them back to midweek services, it becomes a challenge. Another is developing visible leadership roles. As the growth outpaces our infrastructure, we're trying to catch up by creating new opportunities for service.

As a young, new Nazarene African-American pastor, what do you have to say about reaching African-American people?

First, *African-American* and *poor* are not synonymous. As long as we approach ministry with that old paradigm, we're going to miss something. Another thing—our Black and white members will all say they want the same thing from the church. I think that what's most exciting is that it's time to break down some of those old barriers and stereotypes and let go of some old baggage and get excited about what God is doing.

I caution pastors when they talk about reaching out to African-Americans to avoid assuming that they all identify with the urban experience. I believe that dialogue about multicultural ministry will really settle on matters having to do with those that have and those that have not.

You're talking about wealth and poverty.

And that's to me the real cultural divide. In marketing you have multiple cultures—if we don't get that yet, we're missing a real opportunity. I think the real issue that's coming before us is not Black/white but how do people of means connect with those who are disenfranchised whatever color they are. That will become the focal point for Risen Lamb.

Is the church more accepting of differences than the general unchurched population?

The Risen Lamb community certainly is. I don't know that I can speak that way for the church in general. Some people have been shocked that white students would drive out to hear me preach. They didn't quite get that. Here you will really find a spirit of acceptance.

Concluding Thoughts

As I joined in the inspirational, energetic worship at both of these multicultural congregations, I wondered what set them apart. Why have they been able to attract and retain people from such different cultural experiences?

How did Corey and Beth Jones with their original small core group of white members successfully expand their mission to include affluent as well as low-income Black people from the neighborhood around the church?

And how have Dorzell and Beth King been successful in attracting Blacks, whites, and Hispanics from throughout the Kansas City area to a church they would have avoided in the past?

Corey and Dorzell will both say that cultural blending is not a strategy for growing their churches. They are very aware and intentional about what it takes to create an inclusive environment where people from different cultures feel at home. But they almost never draw attention to the differences among them and their outreach is not to people simply because of cultural identities. The cultural balance is the result of something other than trying to be inclusive.

In each congregation I observed something like a spiritual meta-culture. In their worship experiences people were invited to encounter what God was doing among and through them that had little, if anything, to do with the color of their skin, their culture, or their country of origin. The sermons addressed universal human needs. In their testimonies and singing, while giving their offerings, praying, and greeting one another, the pastors and people of these congregations are writing a new story.

Could we be nearing a time when people of all races and languages, particularly those in the Christian family, will want to be reminded that they are more alike than different?

The Fastest-Growing Nazarene Church

Yuba City Church of the Nazarene
Yuba City, California
Gary Moore, Pastor

Profile

Yuba City Nazarene, as they refer to themselves, has been the fastest-growing Church of the Nazarene in the United States for the three-year period ending in 2007. Its Sunday worship attendance has increased to over 2,000, adding approximately 500 annually for three consecutive years.

Pastor Gary Moore, a 60-something veteran missionary and pastor, celebrated his 10th anniversary on the first Sunday of January 2007. Ten years ago when he began here, the church had an average attendance of 250. During his first seven years they experienced good growth with two services in a sanctuary seating 350. In 2003 they built a 13,000-square-foot multiuse Family Life Center. It provides a place for seven-day-a-week athletics and social events as well as seating 650 for Sunday worship. Upon the completion of the new building, their growth accelerated.

Gary is medium height, graying, trim, and athletic looking. His soft-spoken, casual manner belies his intensity and leadership skills in guiding a youthful, creative staff in giving direction to a growing congregation. After graduating from Pasadena College (now Point Loma Nazarene University) in 1969 he pastored in Nebraska for three years, then attended Nazarene Theological Seminary. From there he and his wife, LaVonna, went to Holland to help start a church in Rotterdam. They returned to the United States to serve churches in Idaho and California before going to South Africa, Rwanda, and the Congo for eight more years of missionary work. Returning again to the United States they served a church in Eugene, Oregon, before moving to Yuba City.

Yuba City is a medium-sized town of 50,000, 45 miles north of Sacramento. A few years before he came, the church had relocated from the center of the city to its present 13-acre campus on the western edge of town boarded by light industry, residential housing, and orchards. The most visible building from the road is a modern sanctuary that now serves as the children's ministry center. Located behind the sanctuary and separated by a courtyard is the new Family Life Center.

On that anniversary Sunday I watched the people coming and going as they navigated the crowded parking lot and walked back and forth between the buildings. I wondered how they could continue to grow in this somewhat limited facility. During the service they announced a new worship service in a school building two miles away. A worship leader leads the service with live music, and in keeping with the new multisite trend of establishing video venues, a videotape of Pastor Moore's 8 A.M. sermon is driven to this new site. The congregation watches the sermon on a large screen. On that Sunday Pastor Moore encouraged his people to attend the video venue worship to allow more room for growth at the main campus.

As I talked with Gary and his staff, I was impressed that they are not trying to grow their church. They are trying to accommodate the growth produced by doing lots of things well. And yet I wondered why this is the fastest-growing church in the United States. In part it is the result of excellent pastoral leadership for 10 years. Gary is a very good communicator, a wise elder of sorts with a winsome style who brings much practical wisdom to his sermons. He has a common touch with people. He just looks and sounds like someone you'd enjoy talking to. The worship is energetic yet informal enough to feel relaxed, which is in keeping with the California culture. It's not so much a church trying to be friendly as a group of friendly people enjoying one another and offering hospitality to all their new friends, and that's the same way Gary is.

He has assembled a talented staff that knows how to organize church programs that address the family needs of suburban America. I talked with people between the services for whom this is a neighborhood church—connected to and serving a wide range of local interests. They don't advertise. They just talk about what they enjoy, and others—many others—want to get in on it too.

Conversation with Pastor Gary Moore

What did you find at Yuba City Nazarene when you arrived in 1997?

The church was very unified. They had just moved into their new building—what we now call the Light House. They were really ready to go—very anxious to move out toward a vision. It was running about 250. Even without a paid music leader they were transitioning to a more contemporary worship style. The senior citizens were remarkable. Through the years they haven't necessarily liked all the changes, but their attitude has always been in favor of doing whatever it takes to reach people.

Have you lost people as a result of growth and change?

Very few. I've been extremely blessed. I think that's been a key part, enabling us to get along and grow. We're up to 2,000 in attendance now.

From 250 to 2,000 in 10 years is a steep climb. How do you account for that kind of growth?

When we look for any kind of human element, we'd have to say it's unity; there's been a remarkable sense of unity—everybody's been on the same page. Obviously you have to have good leadership, lay and staff. The Lord's blessed us with that—people who are willing to look forward.

What is the magnet that draws people to Yuba City Nazarene?

There is a sense of excitement and anticipation about God. People sense that when they come. I know a lot of places can be friendly and warm, but I think we're both. And even as we've gotten larger we've striven to still keep a family thing going among ourselves. We have some tremendous ministries going on for youth and children. In our youth ministry we have a youth worship service on Wednesday night because we don't have room for everybody all the time, and it can have up to 400 young people worshipping God—they don't play games or do anything else—almost every week we have young people that come to know the Lord.

When do you worship and what is it like?

Sundays—8:00, 9:30, and 11 A.M. for adult worship, with youth worship on Wednesday night. We just don't have room for all of them together. The three Sunday services are the same. It's fairly contemporary. We have an incredible worship leader. Not every Sunday, but most Sundays there's a hymn worked into the worship package— probably the new people have no idea it's a hymn. It's sung in the style of our other songs. We have a band and choir—it's a large worship team that works for us. It just adds so much energy. It's not the traditional choir with robes and all that kind of stuff. We're participatory—people genuinely enter in. It's not as if they are looking at the worship team for a great performance. We integrate technology with video clips. Most of the time my youth pastor and worship leader create video announcements that are really funny and people laugh; we laugh and have a good time—and we worship. More Sundays than not we have altar calls inviting people to come forward. It's tricky because we have another service following. But we have altar workers and prayer teams who come and take people off to the side.

How would you describe your preaching?

Well, I've always been a biblical preacher with a lot of expositional preaching. My style has changed. I hope my message hasn't, because I really desire to communicate the Word. I know from looking back through the years that I try to include a lot more application. I kind of morphed into not using notes or a pulpit; I try to have nothing between the people and me. I'm not by nature a humorous guy, but I intentionally use humor when I can. I work really hard at knowing the culture and try to know what's going on in people's lives and my own so that I can relate.

What do you mean by culture?

Culture is where we live—where people are here. We're California, but we're not Sacramento or certainly not San Francisco. This was a rural, agricultural area, so there's still a small-town atmosphere that's pretty conservative politically. When you think of California, you might not think that—but here we are up in this valley. And yet we're into all the cultural mores of consumerism and materialism.

What is your target audience?

It has been young families with younger children.

What is the first contact most visitors have with the church?

Most visitors come first to worship, but also some come through the youth ministry and children's outreach. VBS is traditional. The Harvest Fair we have at Halloween has become really big—we can hardly fit it on our campus. Other things such as sports ministries attract visitors, but the majority of new contacts are people who come to worship. We do minimal advertising. We probably have 10 to 15 new families that we know about and get information from each Sunday.

How do you follow up?

I send each family a letter right away. We have a team that within a few days delivers homemade bread to their home. They don't say much other than "Thank you for coming—here's some bread—enjoy it." That's the first-week follow-up. Then we have a newcomer activity between the services or after the third service. It's a chance to get acquainted with the staff. Over the last year we were way behind in connecting people with small groups. We were growing so fast we weren't connecting them.

What are you doing with small groups now?

Over a year ago we did Forty Days of Purpose. We launched small groups through that. Then we brought a small-groups pastor on staff. We'll form a small group around anything that's an interest or passion. We have all kinds of groups—most of them short-term groups. For instance, we have a guy that gives guitar lessons. People come for lessons and then do a study.

What percentage of your attendance is in small groups?

Right now about 40 percent. We've gone from 2 percent. We'd like to connect everybody. I'd like to see it get up there to 75 to 80 percent.

Is adult Sunday School included in your small-group ministry?

Yes and no. We really have a difficult time now with adult Sunday School because of space. We have no room on Sundays for adult Sunday School, so we have to be very creative. We're trying to determine what steps to take in our next building. We're really out of space in so many ways. We have groups meeting on Sunday night that are like Sunday School. The children have Sunday School and worship three times during the adult worship. We have a couple of youth Sunday School classes on Sunday morning.

You have increased 500 for three consecutive years—about 1,500. That's remarkable. How do you assimilate that many people?

We're scrambling all the time. That's why the small groups had to become such a priority. And then we have the three "Cs," as we call them: celebrating, which is worship; connecting, however we can make people feel connected; and commissioning, to be in service and mission. We're just trying to have as many connecting events as we possibly can that will allow people to go beyond just attending worship and get to know some kind of smaller group of people, whatever that is. We try to be very creative in doing that.

What do you tell pastors about how to grow their churches?

One of my deep convictions is that no matter what you do, you can't build and sustain church growth without good, effective preaching. That takes commitment from the preaching pastor. Everything else builds and centers around that. I spend most of my time preparing for sermons.

How much time?

Oh, I don't know. Monday we have a staff meeting and then I use Tuesday to try to get everything centered in my mind and heart and then work on it the rest of the week. I don't know the hours, but it's a constant thing with me. My opinion is that if God has called you to preach, then you can be good. We're not Billy Grahams and all of that, but if He's called you to preach, you can be effective. But you've got to believe in that. For long-term ministry if that element isn't there, you're not going to make it.

How do you plan and prepare for worship?

We spend a lot of time putting that together. I meet with our worship leader and his assistant early in the week. We talk about where we're going, what we're trying to do, the response we're looking for. And then they work together to fill that in with music. We have a theme every week—something people can grab hold of. The themes are built around my preaching. They'll decorate the front of the sanctuary. Last summer we did a series on Sailing the Summer Seas with Paul out of Acts, so we had a big boat up there. They work on integrating a drama or a video clip and sometimes interviews.

We went to two services as we were trying to break the 300 barrier. We found out that we had reached 80 percent capacity in worship, Sunday School, and parking. Having grown up in the Church of the Nazarene all of my life, it was a big philosophical shift at that point, because I had always come to Sunday School at 9:30 A.M. and stayed for church at 11 A.M.—you were there for around 2½ hours. We're now saying we need you to come and then leave so some other people can come. That was a big shift.

Having multiple services has obviously been well received.

Well, yes. It really opened a door. We've now been in the Family Life Center for over three years, which has doubled our worship capacity for each service. We were running just about 700 when we moved, and we've almost tripled in three years.

How is your church organized?

We have a team leadership structure. We elect lay team leaders for various ministries, such as marriage and family, men's and women's ministries, sports, and prayer ministry. We also elect a nine-member administrative committee (also known denominationally as the trustees and stewards); they look after the finances. Staff members work with and oversee the elected team leaders. The administrative team plus elected ministry team leaders meet as the church board every couple of months. Before that, we had a typical church board. It was pretty traditional. You ended up discussing things that didn't have much to do with ministry.

How has your missionary career informed your ministry in Yuba City?

Once you've lived outside the States for a while and you've had to grapple with how culturally involved much of our theology is—I mean the church at large in America, not just the Church of the Nazarene—it makes you see that it is extremely important to bring to people a kingdom of God worldview. For many of our people their concept of God is way off, skewed. Being a missionary has helped me see a wider perspective.

Does it make sense to talk about the United States as a mission field?

It does. Recently my wife and I visited Europe. You see where Europe is now and you hope that's not where we're headed—a post-Christian era.

What's in the future?

We try not to limit God. We have a desire to help plant churches. We have a Korean congregation that meets during the 11 A.M. hour. We have thousands of East Indians in Yuba City, yet I'm not sure we're multicultural. Our Koreans meet by themselves in our choir room. I'm beginning to think we need to worship together. Certainly here there are two other major groups—East Indian and Hispanic. But I don't know what the future looks like.

The Largest Nazarene Church in the United States

Grove City Church of the Nazarene
Grove City, Ohio
Mark Fuller, Pastor

Profile

In 2005, Mark Fuller became the pastor of the largest Nazarene church in the United States following the 16-year tenure of Bobby Huffaker that saw the attendance increase to over 3,000 in the weekend services. Mark came to Grove City after 18 years at the Crossroads church in Phoenix—a church that grew from 300 to over 1,300 and reported increased attendance every year in its 25-year history.

At Grove City he came to a church that has set the pace for many growing churches with its multiple services (Saturday night included) and high-energy worship that uses multiple screens across the front of a stage in a 2,500-seat concert hall auditorium. Its annual Dream Big conferences have attracted from across the country pastors and denominational leaders representing many faith traditions, and its Saturday evening ministry to bikers—motorcyclists that is—on special occasions has attracted thousands.

Located on a city block in the middle of a middle-class suburb south of Columbus, Ohio, the campus has become a gathering place for community activities. Upon entering any one of the several entrances a visitor is guided to the hospitality center, which is situated next to a food court, bookstore, and supervised children's recreation area resembling but larger than any at McDonald's. This part of the church is open every day for neighborhood parents who want to bring their children to play while they enjoy lunch or just be with friends.

When Bobby Huffaker announced his retirement plans nearly a year ahead, he gave the church plenty of time to search for his successor. Eventually Mark Fuller accepted the invitation and began serving immediately following Huffaker's departure.

Mark is a preacher's son. He admits that respect for his father left him with what he experienced as a "debilitating fear" that he, too, would be called to preach. He struggled with that fear until near the end of his education when, he remembers, he found a park bench at seminary after homiletics class and prayed a very simple prayer: "Lord, I don't understand it; I can do a lot of things for You." "But," as Mark relates, "God reminded me that He didn't care what I could do for Him; He wanted to know what I was willing to let Him do through me. God's anointing began to flow through me as I preached from that point on."

After seminary graduation Mark served the youth at Olathe College Church in Kansas, then on to Texas for 5 years before his 18 years at Crossroads in Phoenix.

Conversation with Pastor Mark Fuller

What about the growth at Crossroads during your 18 years?

The church was about 300 when I arrived as the second pastor in 1987. We experienced solid, steady growth—in fact, during its 25 years of existence, Crossroads experienced growth every single year. It never plateaued; it was always looking for the next level—the next opportunity.

What was the attendance when you left?

1,360 was the average for our final year.

How does a church grow every year for 25 years?

Visionary leadership to start with; an understanding of spiritual authority—a willingness to follow the leadership; the people's willingness to change and to accommodate the personal sacrifices needed to make that change; and a vision for the lost.

How did you change?

I spent a lot of time trying to figure out how to grow the church and discovered that the biggest key to growing the church was allowing God to grow me.

In what way?

I had a tremendous fear that if the church began to plateau, maybe I would have to leave. The church experienced growth quickly the first year or two and then it kind of tailed off. I thought maybe I was a three-to-five-year guy—a spark plug who would then go on to the next church and do the same thing. I didn't think I had what it takes to relocate the church if I knew that needed to happen. I didn't think I had what it takes to lead a church of 500, 800, 1,000, or 2,000— whatever the number may be. Dealing with that self-doubt was critical.

How did you get over that?

Out of desperation. John Maxwell came to town teaching his leadership seminar. I thought that this was going to be the key to getting us off high-center—to getting us growing again. I got all my leaders to attend—we even scheduled lunch together—my board members and staff around the table. We had an opportunity to ask John questions. I had the last question, which I thought was the most important. I asked, "What's the key to growing a church past the 500 barrier?" I thought he would say something about having the right staff or lay involvement or getting a building up or something like that.

He pointed his finger right at me and he said, "You." I realized at that moment that it was up to me. Out of desperation I went to my knees. In prayer and the Word I began to ask, "God, what do You want to grow in me. I don't know what it takes to grow the church. I don't think I'll ever know that." I was led to a passage in Exodus where Jethro counsels Moses. As I was reading through that passage I'd read many times before, it seemed that the principles God was wanting to grow in me just leapt off the pages and into my heart.

First, I noticed that Moses was being a prophetic, priestly voice to the people. That was the call to preach, and God reaffirmed that in my own life I was to give my attention to the preaching ministry. Second, Moses was to be the vision-caster—casting God's vision for His people. And that's a big one—being the primary vision-caster for God's people. It's huge—helping every individual understand what that vision is. I realized that a leader cannot delegate that. I began to be open to God teaching me how to cast His vision. Third, Moses appointed different people to lead. To me that was saying I was to invest my life in leaders—to pour my life into leaders.

Those three things became the driving force of my life and ministry: to preach, to cast vision, and to develop leaders. It took me a couple years to incorporate those into my schedule—into my lifestyle. Today I spend 95 percent of my time in those three areas. It's been liberating for me. It was hard—it was very difficult—but allowing God to clarify those things in me was critical to allowing the church to grow. John Maxwell was right when he says that churches are not growing if the pastor is not growing.

During those 18 years you saw many significant shifts in the way churches are organized and how they worship, including the emergence of small groups. How did you adapt to those changes?
Probably one of the biggest changes for the congregation structurally was moving from a board-run to a staff-led church. That was

a difficult transition. As we developed staff to lead in the ministry, there was tension over who was going to set the agenda—the paid staff or church board. In a smaller church the church board represents the leadership and that is what they do. I felt that my role was to bring in the strongest staff I could—as leaders, not just men and women to do ministry. That's a mistake I think a lot of pastors make. They hire staff for a task or a position or a program. I believe you need to find leaders. If you get the right people onboard then the rest—the vision, the direction, the program, everything else—will flow from that. If you don't have strong leaders, your church board is not going to be inclined to release the ministry to them. But if you have strong leaders who have built trust and proven themselves, then a board can more easily release the ministry to the staff. That helps bring about the transition from a board-run to a staff-led church. For a church to pass that 500 mark it has to move to that area.

We had the worship wars the same as everyone else did. But when they called me to be pastor, they made it very clear: "We believe you are the person to teach us how to praise and worship and how to pray." I came with that mandate. When I began to press the envelope and do some things outside the box, the sparks started to fly. I reminded them that that was what they had asked me do. They still continued to support me. We paced it right. That was the key. Leadership is an art. It's like riding a wave—if you've ever done any surfing—you have to adjust your weight as the wave unfolds. Leadership is knowing how to press the envelope and then back away and then press again someplace else.

The church's worship style never crystallized; it always continued to grow. It's like pouring concrete—if you keep moving it, keep working it, you can move it along, but once it sets and gets hard, there's nothing you can do but break it up and start over again.

How does worship at Grove City compare to Crossroads?

Generally the two churches are very similar. I think that that's one of the major reasons why the transition has been so smooth. They are similar in style, but really it's not style that I think is critical when it comes to praise and worship. Praise and worship is more a matter of heart focus than style; it's people gathering together and creating an atmosphere that's conducive to connecting with God in a personal way. The people on the platform are not performers; they're signposts pointing people to God. Praise and worship opens up everything else. It makes people receptive to the ministry of the Word.

How do new people find out about the church?

I think it's the worship services—certainly in the churches I've pastored. In our American church culture that's where you're going to get the biggest bang for your investment of personnel and resources. We did major events at Crossroads, and Grove City does major events. These are community awareness events, and some people do come in through these, but by and large the greatest persistent point of entry for new people in the life of the church is the weekend services. People come to church because they have this God-sized hole in their heart they're trying to fill—a problem in their marriage, a financial issue, or a rebellious child—and underlying all of that is a hunger to connect with God.

Why do think that 80 percent of the churches in the United States and Canada have plateaued or are declining? How do you explain the remarkable growth that you've experienced at both Crossroads and now Grove City?

I'll borrow something from Bobby Huffaker. The most important person on any given weekend is the person who is yet to attend. The focus must be kept on people who are pre-Christians, who are not regular church attendees. Everything—the way you develop staff, build your building, and implement programs—must focus on bringing Christ to a person who doesn't know Him.

What is your target audience?

My target audience when preaching is people who are hungry for God. That's not a particular generation, age-group, or cultural group. I want to create an atmosphere for people who are hungry to connect with God wherever they are on their spiritual journey. We come together to celebrate and affirm what God is doing in our lives. We're not a seeker service—as it's been defined at Willow Creek or Saddleback. What I have felt most comfortable with is creating an atmosphere, a setting, where people seeking to connect with God can do so. George Barna says that a third of the people who go to church say that they've never had a personal encounter with God and half haven't had that kind of encounter in the last year. That's a fundamental goal that I have—a place where people can connect with God.

How do you preach?

I'm an exegetical preacher. Right now I'm preaching verse by verse through the Book of Acts. The challenge is to make it topical and interesting and to present it in bite-size pieces so that people can stay with me. I call it a "church on the move," and I'm dividing it up into different sections—but basically I'm preaching verse by verse. I do that most of the time.

Apart from the content, what is your preaching style?

I'm very conversational. I try to envision sitting down over coffee with people when I'm preaching. I'm not just laid-back; I'm focused on driving home the message, but I also try to think of my next-door neighbor—what he or she would think about the scripture and what questions he or she would be asking—and then try to offer some answers. And I always try to give people an opportunity to respond.

Do you try to get people into small groups?

We're going through a time of restructuring here at Grove City. We want everybody to celebrate God's presence and connect with God's people. I've found there are three basic ways that people connect at Grove City—small groups, ministry teams, and education classes. We call all of them connection groups. We require three things of all connection groups—caring, learning, and serving. We've discovered that one size doesn't fit all when it comes to small groups. We live in a very eclectic culture. People very rarely fit into a cookie-cutter approach. I believe in the importance of small groups. We are becoming a church of connection groups—small groups are just one component of that connection.

What percentage of those attending your weekend service is involved in connection groups?

Probably about half.

You've gotten off to a good start in your first year—I hear that the attendance is up.

We're averaging about two or three hundred over a year ago. That's been really exciting. But the most satisfying part is how quickly the people have embraced our leadership. The staff is united—they're all staying—and the church board has given me permission to lead. That's the single most surprising thing I've experienced. I thought it would take several years to earn my spurs as a pastor. It's been great. With the congregation's blessing about 400 of our people have recently left to start a new church. They have grown to nearly 500, while the main campus has gained back more than was given to start this strong new congregation.

What's the future for Grove City?

The vision is to be a Holiness lighthouse for Christ in central Ohio and to be a ministry training center for the next generation of leaders for the Church of the Nazarene. God determines the purpose of the church—we don't. God has raised this church to be a Holiness church. That doesn't mean we are holier than anybody—but it does mean that we're called to emphasize the person and work of the Holy Spirit in the life of the believer and to live this out in a life of holiness. Evangelism is what holy people do.

The New Miami Heat

Bethany Church of the Nazarene
Miami
Obed and Noemi Jauregui, Pastors

Profile

The Miami Bethany Church of the Nazarene is one of the fastest-growing Hispanic congregations, with over 1,000 men, women, youth, and children attending weekly discipleship prayer groups. Obed and Noemi Jauregui began as pastors at Bethany in 1995 with a congregation of less than 50 members three miles from the Miami International Airport in one of Miami's poorest and most dangerous neighborhoods. The church was started in 1962 by some of the first Cuban immigrants fleeing the revolution.

In 1993, Pastor Mel Santiestaban of the Good Shepherd Church in nearby Hialeah, Florida, sponsored Obed and Noemi—both children of Nazarene pastors in Cuba—to immigrate to the United States as religious workers. As a youth leader Obed was threatened with imprisonment for his aggressive evangelism with Campus Crusade founder Bill Bright, who was accused of being a CIA agent. Obed still can't return to Cuba for fear of arrest.

During their 12 years at Bethany the church has grown steadily. There are now more than 600 members with an average worship attendance of over 700 in two Sunday services and 83 discipleship cell groups that meet throughout the week at the church and in homes. They began reaching this neighborhood with compassionate ministry. Distributing donations of clothing and food from a local food bank established the church as a place for people to come in time of need. They then started visiting door-to-door, introducing themselves and leaving a food gift with a brochure inviting their neighbors to church and offering to help if needed. Their growth has continued as they have learned how to serve people in need and lead them to faith and discipleship.

On the Sunday morning I attended, the 350-seat auditorium was so crowded that some who came late were turned away. The evening service attracted a completely different congregation, comprised for the most part of people who came to receive emergency food and clothing assistance as well as to praise and worship God.

Obed and Noemi Jauregui lead the worship celebrations. I learned afterward that part of their discipleship training is about how to worship. Noemi accompanies from a keyboard while a soloist with a backup praise team leads the congregation in Latino gospel music that has caught on throughout Hispanic churches in the United States.

Obed teaches as he preaches, with his notes and scripture references projected on a large screen. Most everyone I saw had an open Bible, referring back and forth in the Old and New Testaments through dozens of verses and taking notes in three-ring binders spread out in their laps. Obed paced across the platform, urging, instructing, and admonishing with passion and humor. The people listened intently, sometimes laughing and clapping as they followed his notes on the screen, turning the pages of their Bibles and writing in their notebooks.

About an hour after he began preaching the background music began, Bibles and notebooks were closed. We stood as he spoke directly to those who were new to the congregation and had yet to receive Christ. Pastor Obed told me that there are usually about 20 new people in every service. The 12 who came forward were guided to a room where trained leaders explained to them how to accept

Christ. Then an opportunity was provided for members of the church family to come forward to pray for healing and strength. They crowded around the front—some kneeling, others standing— all praying and singing together until the service ended as it began in celebration and praise. There was no benediction as there was no printed order of service. It just started, and when it ended, no one seemed anxious to leave.

Afterward we milled around in an outdoor courtyard enjoying free hot dogs and soft drinks while the kids lined up for their turns in an enclosed jumping room. I wondered how many came hungry and thirsty for more than spiritual food. Whatever the case might be, they all received what they needed.

I noticed the flags when I left—15 flags displayed across the back of the auditorium representing the nations of their people—mostly from Spanish-speaking Caribbean and Central American countries. Pastor Obed estimated that 80 percent of his people are undocumented immigrants from this very transient neighborhood. "We really do need immigration reform," he commented.

Pastor Obed wanted me to understand that while they are far from where they believe they soon will be, their growth is the result of four key components of their strategy: compassionate ministry (organized through their nonprofit organization Miami Bethany Community Services, Inc.), evangelism, prayer, and the Master's Plan of cell-group discipleship training. They have much to learn, he said, but he believes they can reach thousands more through compassion, evangelism, prayer, and discipleship. They will add additional services to accommodate the growing congregation until they find a location large enough for all the people they know are yet to come.

With my lack of Spanish and Pastor Obed's limited English, we talked as best we could—in itself a conversation that says a lot about multicultural America.

Conversation with Pastor Obed Jauregui

What did you do first to get acquainted with the people in this neighborhood?

Compassionate ministries was first. We gave clothing and food—a lot of food from the food bank and donations from churches and other people. That was the first open door for growing the church.

What came next?

The first step was compassion. The second was prayer. The third was evangelism. You can use any tool, any strategy, but if you don't pray, the people never come. We go door-to-door. We train people to leave a gift of food, like bread or juice, and a brochure inviting them to church.

We make contacts that result in conversions through evangelism campaigns, door-to-door calling, and compassionate ministries. Next is to consolidate. When someone makes a decision for Christ, we need to be sure that the decision is real.

Six years ago we discovered the Master's Plan* to disciple converts in cell groups. New converts are now assigned to a leader who calls them within 24 hours, visits within 72 hours at their house or work, and invites them to become members of a discipleship cell group. Each group has a minimum of 4 and a maximum of 12.

We then encourage converts to attend an encounter—a special 48-hour weekend retreat where they experience a total change in their lives. They are expected to complete 12 lessons—4 before, 4 during, and 4 after the encounter on subjects such as deliverance, forgiveness, worship, and the vision of the church.

How do you train leaders for the discipleship cell groups?

I train and lead the men's groups, my wife leads the women's groups,

---

*A disciple-making strategy originating in South America.

and our youth and children's pastors lead cell groups for youth and children. We now have 85 groups including men, women, youth, and children. The cell-group leaders must complete our School of Leadership, a year-long training program in doctrine and evangelism. About 300 people have completed the leadership training.

What would you say to others who want to learn from your success?

They would be mistaken to think that the discipleship cell groups are enough. The compassionate element is fundamental. And the prayer covenant that we have implemented with the people of the church is as important as the others. Something else that is fundamental for the growing of the church is strengthening of the leaders. We haven't seen the growth that we would like to see. Our biggest challenge is the preparation of the leaders. Only 30 percent of the members of the church have enrolled in the School of Leadership, and not all of them will get to be leaders.

What is your vision for the future?

We would like to see a revival to reach 15,000 people. We are praying for the arena where the Miami Heat basketball team used to play. For now that's the goal.

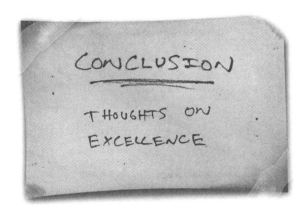

CONCLUSION

THOUGHTS ON EXCELLENCE

During my visit to the Miami Bethany church, I was given several full-color brochures with professional photos and engaging articles describing the church's various programs. It wasn't what I expected from a congregation made up mainly of poor, undocumented immigrants from the Caribbean and Central America. On the other hand, it was consistent with the quality of excellence I've found in growing churches.

Churches don't have to be large or wealthy to grow; they just need to be good. Even small churches can organize worship committees, plan ahead, and rehearse and debrief their worship services. Pastors of all churches can prepare and become good communicators. Small churches may be better at hospitality.

Large, growing churches have been likened to Wal-Mart, growing by taking members from the small churches. But recent studies indicate that churches of all sizes in proximity to large churches may prosper rather than decline. Some unchurched people who are attracted to large churches realize that they prefer the intimate fellowship of a small, healthy church. Megachurches may become feeders for the smaller churches around them.

In his presentations to the 2004 PALCON (regional conferences for Nazarene clergy) noted church growth consultant and author Kennon Callahan told of a conversation he had with a pastor whose small church was in the shadow of a megachurch. Callahan told this pastor who felt threatened by his larger church neighbor, "Be at peace, they can't compete with you," by which he meant that small churches have strengths and advantages of their own, as he develops in his book *Small, Strong Congregations: Creating Strength and Health for Your Congregation.*[1]

I asked a district superintendent what he learned from spending several months of his sabbatical on a tour of America's great churches. He replied that in every instance he noticed excellence in the attention given to amenities such as parking lots, bathrooms, and nurseries as well as the music and preaching. He then observed, "We have a crisis of excellence among many churches on my district."

Quality alone won't produce growth, but of all the other best practices of growing churches there may be none more important than excellence. Excellence in growing churches is about doing things well because the mission and the message of the gospel are important enough to deserve our best.

Introduction

1. George G. Hunter, *Church for the Unchurched* (Nashville: Abingdon, 1996).

2. Reggie McNeal, *The Present Future: Six Tough Questions for the Church* (San Francisco: Jossey-Bass, 2003).

3. George Barna, *Revolution* (Wheaton, Ill.: Tyndale House, 2005).

4. Paul Borden, *Hit the Bullseye* (Nashville: Abingdon Press, 2003).

5. Thom Rainer and Eric Geiger, *Simple Church* (Nashville: Broadman and Holman, 2006).

6. Alan Roxburgh and Fred Romanuk, *The Missional Leader: Equipping Your Church to Reach a Changing World* (San Francisco: Jossey-Bass, 2006).

Chapter 1

1. Christopher E. Bogan and Michael J. English, *Benchmarking for Best Practices: Winning Through Innovative Adaptation* (New York: McGraw-Hill, Inc., 1994).

Chapter 2

1. Joseph B. Pine II and James H. Gilmore, *The Experience Economy: Work Is Theatre and Every Business a Stage* (Boston: Harvard Business School Press, 1999).

Chapter 3

1. John Carver, *Boards That Make a Difference: A New Design for Leadership in Nonprofit and Public Organizations* (San Francisco: Jossey-Bass, 1997).

Conclusion

1. Kennon L. Callahan, *Small, Strong Congregations* (San Francisco: Jossey-Bass, 2000).